Praise for  MW00640468

"**Workplace Gold** is the gold standard for supervisors in law enforcement. Every Chief of Police should have this book and its contents in the hands of their leaders. Well worth making the investment in your department which will definitely pay dividends on the road to excellence".

Chief Dave Jernigan (FBI Special Agent, Ret.)
Madison Police Department, Alabama

"Look no further for a law enforcement leadership development book that can easily translate into promotional exam content. **Workplace Gold** provides emerging and seasoned supervisors with the necessary steps to finding success in their leadership journeys. This book inspires you to think differently about your obligations as a leader and is precisely what I was looking for to move my agency forward."

Chief Melanie Bevan, Ed.D.
Bradenton Police Department, Florida

"**Workplace Gold** is a must read for all supervisors, regardless of rank. Chief Glidden's points are right on target and whether you are holding rank for the first time or a senior manager, his book highlights the key concepts every boss should follow."

Sheriff Kevin F. Coppinger
Essex County Sheriff's Department, Massachusetts

"Show me a problem in American Law Enforcement today (including many currently in the news) and I will show you a "proximate cause" of "X". Too often the "real problem lying in wait" is a supervisor not behaving like a supervisor—or in the alternative a supervisor who tried to behave like a supervisor and was not supported by management. *Workplace Gold* is an excellent primer for every new supervisor—and will benefit veteran supervisors and managers who have the guts to make things better in their agency—and positively impact our profession".

Gordon Graham
Graham Research Consultants

"*Workplace Gold* provides the tools, tips and strategies necessary for becoming or excelling as a successful leader. It specifically focuses in on the one trait all leaders must exhibit and foster, a culture of trust. This is a must read for the entire chain of command in any organization."

Terrence M. Cunningham, Chief of Police (Ret)
Deputy Executive Director
International Association of Chiefs of Police

Workplace Gold

*Strategies for Improving Employee
Morale, Accountability, and Performance*

Workplace Gold

Strategies for Improving Employee Morale, Accountability, and Performance

Chief Ronald C. Glidden (Ret.)

Gold Badge Publishing

Printed in the United States of America.

First printing, August 2020

ISBN: 978-0-578-69723-9

Published by:
Gold Badge Publishing
PO Box 73
South Wellfleet, MA 02663
www.ronglidden.com

Dedication

This book is dedicated to my father, Charles S. Glidden, Jr., who died in 2020. In addition to a successful business career, he served his community as a deputy sheriff, a reserve police officer, and a director of emergency management. As a patrol sergeant, I had the unique opportunity and privilege to be an instructor when my father was training to become a reserve police officer. However, throughout my life, he was the real instructor and my role model. He led by example and always demonstrated character, integrity, a strong work ethic, and a commitment to lifelong learning. Most importantly, he taught me the importance of serving others.

Contents

Acknowledgments

Thank you to our nation's law enforcement professionals who put their lives on the line every day to keep us safe. Thank you, also, to my seminar and conference attendees and my weekly *Bulletproof Leadership Tip* subscribers. Your support, frequent questions, and continual feedback have made this book possible. Also, a special thank you to Gordon Graham and Jack Enter. You were the first two leadership speakers to whom I had the privilege of listening to after becoming a police chief in 1994. You influenced both my law enforcement and speaking careers.

Introduction

When I first began writing this book, my memory flashed back to 1990, when I was working as a patrol sergeant. I wrote an article for *POLICE* magazine about Joseph Wambaugh. Wambaugh is a former LAPD Detective Sergeant and a best-selling author of numerous books, including novels such as *The Blue Knight, The New Centurions,* and *The Choirboys,* and nonfiction books such as *The Onion Field,* and *Echoes in the Darkness.*

I had the pleasure of interviewing Wambaugh for the article, and we talked about the characters in his books. He wrote about officers who were sarcastic, cynical, occasionally in trouble, suspicious of their administration, not always appreciated by their immediate supervisors, and sometimes treated unfairly by their departments. Some of his characters were clearly problem employees, and not all their problems were fictional. When I asked about those problems, Wambaugh said that not all the dangers officers face come from the street.

In writing *The Onion Field*, Wambaugh said he met Karl Hettenger—the surviving officer from the Onion Field incident. He said the department's insensitive treatment drove the guilt-ridden Hettenger over the edge and he was ultimately fired after a shoplifting incident. In writing his nonfiction book, *Echoes in the Darkness*, Wambaugh talked about how Sergeant Joe Van Nort became so obsessed and frustrated working a murder case that it led to his fatal heart attack. Wambaugh told me he thought officers should *keep investigations (and the job) in perspective, and that family, career, and even health have to be considered.* Recalling Wambaugh's words, I could not help thinking about the role that leadership plays in the overall wellbeing of law enforcement employees.

Throughout my law enforcement career, I worked for and observed many types of leaders. A few even seemed to come from the pages of Wambaugh's books. Some were excellent role models, who cared about their employees. Others were poor examples to follow. When I became a supervisor, I tried to emulate the positive examples as much as possible. I felt privileged to lead so many talented and dedicated employees, who made my job easy and enjoyable. However, there were also a few employees who challenged my skills and my patience. And more than once, I thought Wambaugh should have talked to a few of those employees to get material for another bestseller. Some employees made me doubt both my leadership abilities and even my decision to accept a leadership position.

Law enforcement leaders today experience the same challenges. They work with an extremely diverse group of individuals. To get the best performance from those individuals, they need sound leadership strategies that are more than mere theory. They need practical tools that can be applied in a wide range of both routine and emergency situations. I wrote this book to provide law enforcement leaders, like you, with a starting point in identifying such strategies.

Before I continue, please heed these words of caution. The employees you manage and supervise, early in their careers, became very skilled at reading people. They are skilled at reading, not only people they encounter in public, but also their coworkers and supervisors. They can spot insincerity at a distance and are skilled at knowing when someone is trying to manipulate them. They also have a well-developed BS indicator. Because of this, please note that nothing in these pages is intended to suggest that you try to trick or manipulate any employee. This book provides no quick fixes, miracle cures, tricks, or techniques. As a minimum, techniques feel insincere. At worst, they feel like manipulation. And if employees think you are trying to manipulate them, you will lose their trust.

My goal in writing this book is to provide practical leadership strategies to law enforcement leaders. Rather than listing individual ranks, I use the term *supervisor* throughout the book for the sake of convenience to refer to anyone with supervisory responsibilities. The strategies included here work for any executive, manager, or supervisor (regardless of rank) who wants to improve employee morale, accountability, and performance.

Strategies differ from techniques. They are not magical elixirs that require no effort. Rather, they are a process that will assist leaders in making long-term changes to their leadership efforts to help create a better work environment.

Making these changes will help leaders create a work environment where employees treat each other with dignity and respect; where most employees enjoy coming to work; where motivation can flourish; where job satisfaction improves; and where individuals have the opportunity to reach their full potential. Strategies work because they become part of who a supervisor is, both as a person and as a leader. These strategies are most effective when a supervisor makes the conscious decision to become a committed student of leadership and strives to continually improve their leadership ability throughout their career.

I hope that the strategies in this book help you in your leadership endeavors. Whether what you read is fresh information to you, serves as a reminder of something you have heard before, or just affirms that what you are doing right now in your leadership effort is a sound strategy, I hope you find value in reading this book.

Read and reread this book as often as needed to provide yourself either with reminders on what to do, or confirmation that you are doing an excellent job—even on days when you question your own ability. Mark this book up with a highlighter, underline sentences, which are important to you, in ink, and make notes in the book's margin. And when one of your subordinates asks you to pass down your well-worn and marked-up copy of this book so they could learn to be a leader like you, do him or her a favor and buy that future leader their own copy. Get them started being a committed student of leadership. That is what genuine leaders do!

CHAPTER 1

Individuals

The public usually thinks of law enforcement professionals as a single group of people, identical in every respect. Law enforcement leaders often share that same perception. It is a perception that can cause problems for supervisors at every level of their organization.

Same from the Start—Almost
A quick overview of the law enforcement hiring process makes it easy to understand why people assume that law enforcement employees are all the same. Any law enforcement job requires certain educational requirements. Applicants all undergo a rigorous background check that looks for disqualifying criminal behavior and noncriminal character flaws. Many applicants undergo a psychological evaluation. All applicants undergo a job interview. The process is designed to weed out potential problem employees, leaving only suitable candidates.

Similar Training—Similar Screening

Successful candidates enter a police academy or similar training. In theory, the training weeds out problem recruits. But the weeding-out process during training can be flawed. Problem recruits sometimes become problem full-time employees.

After graduation from formal training, the employee enters semiformal on-the-job training, where the new employee receives instruction, mentoring, and coaching from an experienced employee. A Field Training Officer or FTO may serve in that role and serve as another level in the vetting process. At least part of that process should determine if the new employee is ready to engage in routine work, needs additional training, or is unsuitable for permanent employment. Flaws in this process exist whenever FTOs fail to recognize their duties.

After completing the FTO program or other on-the-job training, the employee completes a probationary period, during which he or she is observed by supervisors and coworkers. This vetting process, too, can be flawed when supervisors either fail to supervise or avoid the conflict necessary to correct or at least document problem behavior. Problem probationary employees are rarely cured of their problem behaviors just because their probation ends. They often become permanent employees with chronic problems.

The Same Everything Else—Sort of

In theory, every employee who works for a law enforcement organization must meet the same minimum standards for being hired, the same initial formal training, the same on-the-job training, after which, every employee follows the same rules, regulations and policies, and even wears the same uniform. Supervisors expect the same minimum performance standards and same appropriate behavior from all employees. It is natural then to assume that all employees are similar, if not identical. You might even assume that to avoid allegations of favoritism, you must treat everyone the same. Many supervisors believe that treating everyone alike is the only way to be fair. They might be correct—if all employees were truly identical.

Employees Are Individuals

Let me be clear about this. If you treat all employees alike, you will alienate about 75% of your workforce. And those who feel alienated will believe they are being treated unfairly. Despite a similar or even identical hiring and training process; and despite dressing employees alike; requiring them to follow identical rules, regulations, policies and procedures; and despite your personal expectations for their behavior and performance, they are all different from each other. Your employees are individuals.

Individuals had unique backgrounds before they came on the job. They had different parents, teachers, and life experiences. Some are more educated than others. Some have military experience. They possess unique personalities. Different factors influence their morale, and different internal and external factors influence their motivation. Some are introverts and some are extroverts. Some worry too much, and some seldom worry about anything. Some shine when working with groups, and others excel when working alone. Some are star performers right from the beginning, and some are slow starters, but are willing learners with potential. Some employees seem incapable of giving you maximum effort. Others will give you a 100% effort, but their maximum effort might result in them being just an average worker. Not that average is horrible, but it is important for you to know that not every employee has the desire, potential, or ability to become a motivated superstar. Some will be solid performers with little effort on your part, and some will require your maximum leadership (and management) effort—just to help them maintain minimum standards.

> *Getting the desired performance from individuals might require a slightly different leadership strategy for each employee.*

It is essential to remember that getting the desired performance from individuals might require a slightly different leadership strategy for each employee. Building trust is an individual concept. You earn trust in some employees by providing professional development and career mentoring. But, with an employee who cares little about career advancement, you might have better success at earning trust by having casual conversations about their family and hobbies. Each individual employee is unique.

Likewise, some employees will respond better to a particular communication style. Some might thrive on your continual feedback, while another employee views your feedback as excessive and a form of micromanagement. Some will appreciate your humor, and others will view it as demeaning. Some employees need, desire (and even crave) more feedback than others.

Even how you give recognition or criticism might need modification depending on the individual employee. To get the best performance out of your employees, understand that one size does not fit all. Your job as a supervisor is to determine which set, or combination of leadership strategies, works best for individual employees to help you get the best performance from everyone.

CHAPTER 2

The Morale Killers

There are certain performance results that you desire and certain results that the public demands. Besides performance results, today, the public demands more accountability and more transparency than ever before. And if those thoughts do not keep you up at night, I am guessing you have one or two employees who cause you a little concern, and maybe an occasional sleepless night. I call these employees *morale killers*.

It is a safe bet that you can name your #1 morale killer. They are not easily forgotten. I am not talking about someone who is an occasional annoyance. Nor am I talking about someone you wish would show just a little more initiative. I am talking about that employee who sucks every bit of enjoyment out of your job.

Your #1 morale killer is that one employee you talk about almost every night at home over dinner. They give you a headache thinking about them before you even arrive at work in the morning. When you arrive at work and see their car is not in the parking lot, all you can think of is how relieved you are that you do not have to deal with them today.

Morale killers can be found everywhere—in every size organization. They thrive on negativity and promote low morale. There are days when it feels like their negativity is so consuming that it sucks all the oxygen out of a room. And their negativity can spread like a virus. They cause reduced productivity, burnout, stress, sick-time abuse, employee turnover, conflicts between coworkers, and negative interactions with the public. They undermine your leadership efforts. They complain and they blame. In short, they drain your energy and your organization's resources.

It Is Not About Rank

When I first started teaching my *Bulletproof Leadership* class, my intent was to provide supervisors with strategies on how to deal with their morale-killing subordinates. It did not take long before seminar attendees started complaining about their morale killers who were not always their subordinates. In some cases, their #1 morale killer was their supervisor. Clearly, rank is not an indicator of who is, or is not, a morale killer.

Morale killers come in all ranks. They do not get cured just because they get promoted. Some people get promoted because they are excellent test-takers. Some get promoted because they had exceptional technical skills in their old job—an old job that required no people skills. Once promoted, they find the technical skill is not as important as it once was, and a high degree of people skills and emotional intelligence is needed. At this point, some of those newly promoted individuals get the training they need or become quick on-the-job learners who develop a new appropriate set of leadership and people skills. They lose their morale-killing tendencies.

People can certainly change, but they must want to change. Unfortunately, many morale killers (of all ranks) fail to see a need to change—even when instructed to change. Good leadership can influence some people to want to change, but others will resist that influence. For those unwilling to change, all the training in the world will not matter. There are supervisors who display wall-to-wall training certificates in their office, but who are morale killers who mistakenly assume their rank and training certificates alone will build employee trust. They refuse to change their demeaning and micromanaging, or conflict-avoidance, morale-killing behavior. They do their subordinates and their organization a grave injustice.

Change What You Can Change

With your subordinates, you have at least some ability to require a change. You can accomplish this in one of two ways. First, you can lead them in such a way that you build trust and commitment. Your charisma, communication style, and knowledge of trust-building strategies certainly helps. Employees ideally become loyal, dedicated, hardworking, and committed—at least to you, if not the organization. And for those subordinates who are not swayed by your great leadership efforts or personal charisma, you outrank them. You have *positional authority*. If need be, you can compel a subordinate's compliance to a minimum standard. It is not the best option for achieving peak performance, but at least it is an option.

For those coworkers who are the same rank as you and over whom you possess no positional authority, you are left with only *personal authority*. That means you can influence, but not compel. The better work relationship you build with that person, the better chance you have of influencing their behavior. But they could still refuse your advice and resist your influence.

Sometimes the behavior of a coworker of the same rank can cause you problems with your subordinates. Your coworker might make public comments about his or her belief that you are too harsh

> The application of any leadership strategy needs to be tempered by the reality of managing a real police department with real problems.

on your subordinates or too "by the book." Such comments can easily undermine your leadership efforts. It is important to understand that you must do what is right for you and your subordinates.

What is right is not always the easiest or most popular course of action. And just because something works for another supervisor does not mean it is right for you or your subordinates. You can influence, but you cannot control other supervisors of the same rank. If you cannot influence them to your way of thinking, at least try to convince them to supervise their subordinates however they see fit, but to allow you to do the same with your subordinates. Differences in opinion and even debates are fine between supervisors. But try to establish a mutual agreement not to undermine each other in front of the other's subordinates.

When They Outrank You

The morale killers who outrank you pose the most significant challenge. You have no positional authority over such individuals. Your best hope of influencing them (for both the organization and your subordinates) is to establish a strong working relationship with them in advance.

If you were making some critical leadership mistakes that were hurting employee morale and performance, you might benefit from a subordinate who had the courage to give you feedback. You could then make a change—if you determined it was needed. Your supervisor or boss deserves the same courtesy and courage from you.

You will sometimes encounter a morale-killing boss who, not only refuses to acknowledge any mistakes were made, but clearly does not want your feedback. They might even demean your attempt to offer such feedback. If you work under those conditions, please do not give up. Your subordinates need you. They need a positive role model. They need you for guidance, feedback, and recognition. And sometimes they need you to run interference so that their negative interaction with your morale-killing boss is minimal. You might be the one positive influence in their lives within your organization. Do not give up on them just because you work for a morale killer. Show them that genuine leaders are not morale killers.

CHAPTER 3

The Secrets of People Management

There are three secrets of people management that are the foundation of all leadership strategies. These are not novel ideas. People often assume if a concept is old that it cannot work as well as a new trendy and complex concept. They would be wrong.

You would be hard-pressed to find an entirely new leadership concept in the last 30 years—at least not one that works. I make no claims that the leadership concepts and strategies I advocate throughout this book are new. Neither are they complex. In fact, some might call them basic. I like basic. Basic is easy to explain and easy to apply.

What you read here is not a complex theory conceptualized by professors in the halls of academia. These are practical strategies based on what I believe will work for most supervisors (regardless of rank) in most situations. I base that belief partially on my own experience, training, and research. What convinces me even more about the validity of these leadership strategies is the anecdotal experiences I was privileged to hear from hundreds, if not thousands, of supervisors who have attended my training presentations. Their best experiences with their supervisors always revolved around the practical application of sound basic leadership strategies.

The three secrets of people management are not really secrets. They only seem like secrets because they are so often missed by leaders searching for a more complex new idea or a recent trend complete with all the latest buzzwords. These concepts remain secret when leaders ignore the usefulness of these practical leadership building-blocks. I call them secrets here only because it brings more attention to their importance. Here are the so-called secrets for your consideration.

1. **Everyone wants to feel important.** Not everyone has the opportunity, or even desire, for promotion to the position of supervisor. But employees know that people they perceive as important in their organization get treated differently. They see important people in the workplace treated with professionalism, courtesy, dignity, and respect. Every employee, regardless of rank or position, would like to be treated with that same professionalism, courtesy, dignity, and respect.

2. **No one wants to look stupid.** You may have heard that public speaking is the greatest fear in America. As a professional speaker, I do not agree. I believe that the greatest fear is embarrassing yourself and looking stupid while public speaking. Making

someone feel stupid by demeaning them when they make a mistake is the quickest way to kill both morale and motivation. Everyone makes mistakes, but supervisors who demean employees teach them only to avoid their supervisor rather than learn from their mistakes. Effective leaders hold employees accountable without demeaning or embarrassing them or making them feel stupid.

3. **Everyone wants to be appreciated.** Employees do not need a participation trophy for doing their job. But most would feel more committed to their supervisor if they felt valued and appreciated by that supervisor. Leaders who show appreciation for their subordinates' efforts, and recognize behavior they want repeated, are rewarded by their employees with trust, loyalty, and commitment.

Almost every leadership strategy you will ever hear or read about (including those in this book) is based in part on these three secrets of people management. Do not allow these three concepts to remain secret from those you supervise. Keep them in mind as you start your leadership journey.

CHAPTER 4

Compliance Versus Commitment

Over the past 30-plus years, most law enforcement organizations have worked hard to become more professional. To accomplish this, they have developed countless policies and procedures, as well as rules and regulations. While written guidelines are needed, there is an unfortunate consequence from overemphasizing the written word. That consequence is called compliance.

Compliance

Compliance might sound like something virtuous—a worthwhile achievement. Organizations need standards, but should (or even can) they expect more from employees than mere compliance to those minimum standards? That is a valid question that faces supervisors of all ranks.

The concept of "good enough" typifies the attitude associated with compliance. Unfortunately, many organizations have built a workplace culture based on compliance. They encourage employees to meet the organization's minimum standards, and there is often little incentive for supervisors to encourage employees to exceed those standards. Many employees have learned the hard way that trying to exceed minimum standards by being creative or coming up with new ideas can cause frustration, disappointment, and even chastisement from coworkers and supervisors.

Some employees have learned that going outside narrowly defined operational parameters (trying to do something better or different) can cause mistakes. Mistakes can lead to demeaning criticism or even reprimand. To avoid the risk of mistakes, or to avoid chastisement or embarrassment, for suggesting anything outside the norm, employees find a comfort zone in low-profile mediocrity. Their goal becomes avoiding mistakes, rather than seeking improved results. They seek to meet the organization's minimum requirements and the minimum expectations of their supervisors.

The result is that employees have learned to follow the letter of a written policy to avoid problems with no concern for the intent or purpose of the policy. Employees can become skilled at finding certain words written, or absent, in a policy that absolve them from consequences when a supervisor tries to hold them accountable. These employees become experts at finding loopholes. Unfortunately, their self-serving attempts to avoid consequences often result in the administration writing new policies to fill those loopholes.

Traditional Leadership

You may have known a so-called traditional leader in your career who ruled by the use of fear. I will leave it to you to decide if that supervisor was just results-driven, or whether the supervisor was intentionally tyrannical, vindictive, or mean-spirited. In either case, traditional leadership as used in this context is not synonymous with effective leadership.

In the early 20th century, there were a few financial titans who serve as classic examples of traditional leadership. Those early barons of American industry believed in achieving their desired results at all costs. They were innovators responsible for advancing technology and building enormous financial empires—significant results by most standards. Unfortunately, a quick check of historical facts and anecdotal evidence shows that these successful task-focused wizards of industry and finance were ruthless when dealing with their employees. Their financial success came in spite of, rather than because of, their autocratic and demeaning leadership styles.

Not Extinct but Should Be

In the early to mid-1900s, employees tolerated callous and ruthless treatment from their bosses because they had few other economic options. They labored long hours under deplorable conditions, working for insensitive and demeaning supervisors because they had few choices. Employees met the minimum standard required for the job or they were terminated. If they complained, they were terminated. If they suggested change or improvement in safety measures, or even pointed out mistakes, they were terminated. They toiled and eked out an existence in an atmosphere of fear of their supervisors and their employer. To survive traditional leadership, they became compliant. They were expendable and easily replaced, and so they did exactly what was expected of them—no more, no less.

The word compliant, when used to describe an employee working for a so-called traditional leader, does not imply a horrible employee. Rather, it describes an employee who does what is required to survive in a job— often out of financial necessity.

A Different World Today

Most of us live in a different world today. The tyrannical treatment by so-called traditional leaders of the early 20th century in most cases would not be tolerated today. Unfortunately, a few such leaders still exist. It is not surprising that they often find themselves the subject of management studies started by their municipality to investigate complaints from employees. Such studies sometimes result in termination of the "traditional leader," or in expensive lawsuits against the organization. Besides the obvious perils and ineffectiveness of leadership styles that use fear and intimidation to achieve compliance, today, more than compliance is needed from employees. Law enforcement supervisors need employees who do what is expected of them, but who also do what is right—all the time. They need employees who think and make sound decisions even when there is no policy. And they need employees to make appropriate decisions even when there is no supervisor looking over their shoulder.

Yes, a few so-called traditional leaders remain today: their demeaning, micro-managing, aloof, or self-centered behaviors create workplace cultures where new ideas, creativity, and innovation are stifled. Employees remain silent out of fear, distrust, or disinterest even in the face of potentially catastrophic mistakes or unethical behavior. As a supervisor, you cannot afford compliance. You need commitment.

Commitment

Achieving the desired results from employees will require more than compliance. Even well-meaning, task-oriented supervisors who care for their employees, but lack the skills to show it, will seldom ever achieve those desired results. Supervisors who understand the importance of engaging with employees and earning their trust have a much better chance of earning employee commitment.

> *Committed employees do what is right and do more than is required—even when no one is looking.*

Why does commitment matter? It matters because committed employees do more than is required. They understand the organization's mission and their role in accomplishing that mission. They understand that there is more to their job than avoiding mistakes, finding loopholes in policy, and maintaining a low profile. Committed employees do what is right because it is right, not because they fear their supervisor.

Committed employees do what is right even when no one is looking.

When it comes to commitment, one of the most important things every supervisor should know is that employees are not necessarily committed to the profession. They may, or may not, be committed to the organization. They may not love every aspect of their job or their current assignment. They may not even like all their supervisors or all their coworkers. Employees become committed to one or more individual supervisors. They become committed to a supervisor who has made a difference in their life and who has somehow influenced their morale and motivation. Commitment can never be forced: it must be earned. Smart supervisors earn commitment by building (and earning) trust, by communicating clearly, by holding people accountable, by providing continuous feedback, and by giving recognition to those doing a competent job.

Make no mistake, earning employee commitment takes effort, but it is an effort well worth the time invested. There is no guarantee, even with a lot of hard work by a knowledgeable, well-meaning supervisor, that commitment will be achieved from every single employee. There are those *morale killers* in every workplace who seem resistant to the well-meaning intentions and continuous efforts of even the best leaders. But imagine what a supervisor could accomplish with just one or two more committed employees. Just a few committed employees can make a significant difference—and make the life of a supervisor just a little easier.

CHAPTER 5

Morale

Morale is the general feeling that employees have about their work, their organization, their leaders, and even their coworkers. High morale, when achieved, can lead to improved employee enthusiasm, confidence, job satisfaction, commitment, and performance. Most supervisors would agree that there appears to be a direct link between morale and job performance.

While employee morale is important, supervisors do not always hold absolute control over that morale. Employees encounter diverse issues or problems, both at home and work, over which supervisors retain little or no control. Family issues, relationship issues, medical issues, mental health issues, financial issues, drug and alcohol problems, and a host of other problems can directly affect an employee's morale. In addition, conflicts with coworkers and bosses, or a long-past perceived injustice by a supervisor can all contribute to morale problems.

There are also situations where a supervisor might want to help, but where doing so is beyond the supervisor's ability. A supervisor might wish they could grant subordinates a pay raise, or provide them with the latest, greatest, and newest equipment to make their job easier (and reduce their complaints). But sometimes supervisors can do little more than suggest or advocate for such improvements.

Leaders frequently get the blame for an employee's low morale, but morale is an employee's responsibility. Individuals are responsible for their own morale. An employee might occasionally become angered or disappointed by a supervisor. But a supervisor's poor leadership practices should not govern an employee's emotions, work ethic, or character—at least not over the long term. Supervisors and subordinates alike should never let another person possess that much control over their lives.

One cautionary note before I move on from the subject of morale responsibility. When your subordinates come to you complaining about a problem or issue affecting their morale, please do not tell them it is their responsibility. It is one thing to understand the concept of morale responsibility and another entirely to come across like you do not care about their morale or the issues influencing their morale. Some of their complaints may be legitimate. Listen to their concerns and fix what you can fix.

Morale and the Work Environment
Although factors outside of work can play a role in employee morale, the most significant factor affecting morale is the work environment. But too often, people think of the work environment as the building they work in,

their office, their equipment, the vehicle they drive, or other physical resources.

The work environment can even include overtime issues. Some employees might develop low morale because they are forced to work too much overtime. Others experience morale issues because they do not feel they get enough overtime. Even a nagging computer problem, or the absence of paper for the printer, can be a work environment issue that temporarily influences morale. Unfortunately, supervisors may not enjoy complete control over all the resources on the job. They can recommend, suggest, and advocate, and can even occasionally make the requested improvements happen. But they may not always possess the authority to make every requested purchase, improvement, or change to the physical work environment.

The Work Environment You Create

While you may not always control the equipment and resources in the physical work environment, there is one area over which you have considerable, if not complete, control. You control the work environment that you create. You control your interactions with your subordinates. To a

> *You control the work environment that you create, and that environment influences employee morale.*

large degree, you control their perceptions about your character, integrity, and work ethic. You control how you hold yourself and others accountable. You control whether the workplace—at least while you are present—is a safe environment where coworkers are treated with dignity and respect by you and all other employees.

Unfortunately, because employees are individuals, not every well-meaning word or action on your part will influence everyone's morale. In fact, sometimes you will engage in a behavior that you are certain will result in better morale for everyone, and it seems to result in no perceptible improvement. Fixing the air-conditioning in an employee's vehicle, making sure there is paper for the printer, or holding a problem employee accountable are issues that should be addressed. Supervisors should understand that while addressing those problems will not always result in a miracle cure for everyone's morale, ignoring any problem, legitimate concern, or complaint will hurt employee morale.

A last thought on morale—your morale. It is important to know that as a supervisor, you are onstage the moment you set foot in the workplace. Sometimes you are onstage even when you are not at work. Your morale, or at least their perception of your morale, influences their morale.

CHAPTER 6

Motivation

It is often said that leaders do not motivate employees, but help employees motivate themselves. While motivation is an individual responsibility, it would be helpful for supervisors to know how motivation works. A lack of motivation can be contagious, and there are a lot of factors that can contribute to demotivation. Removing a demotivating factor will not always increase motivation. Improving motivation requires additional effort.

External Motivators

External motivators include tangibles like pay, promotions, commendations, and equipment to name a few. Depending on where you are in your organization's hierarchy, these motivators may be beyond your ability to provide to your employees. There are a few external motivators, however, that are within your control. Keeping employees informed about things that affect their job, coaching, and career mentoring are external motivators available to any supervisor. Providing—or at least recommending—professional development opportunities is another external motivator for some employees. External motivators are things that you can provide to your employees by your words or actions.

What makes motivating subordinates so difficult is that fulfilling an external need for one employee may not fill the need of others. One employee could suggest that the department change to a different uniform hat, choose a new sidearm, adopt a new uniform patch, or change the color of the patrol vehicles. The change might influence the motivation of the employee who suggested it but may do nothing for the motivation of others. But if the change is needed, or at least is not a flawed idea, the fact that you listened to the employee may be more of a motivational factor than the actual change. Improved motivation often develops in one person at a time.

Internal Motivators

Internal motivators are the unseen internal factors that contribute to an employee's motivation. Curiosity can motivate an employee because it encourages the employee to explore new tasks and new assignments. Curiosity can even push an employee just for the pleasure of learning and mastering a new skill or different aspect of the job.

Challenges can motivate employees and push them towards their maximum potential by raising the bar—their own standards—as they work towards a meaningful goal. Those challenges might include personal growth or professional development opportunities.

The desire to possess at least some measure of control over what happens to them is another powerful motivator for employees. They want to be part of the decisions that affect their work, their careers, and their lives.

Employees want to feel appreciated and recognized for their work efforts. The desire for that recognition coming from both their supervisors and peers can be a strong motivator, even if the recognition is only informal or comes in the form of increased respect for their expertise.

Many employees are motivated by the satisfaction they get from belonging to a group. This is especially true in law enforcement. A certain bond of camaraderie (even a family-like feeling) exists with others in the same organization or even the same profession. This

> *It's not your job to motivate others. It's your job to create a work environment where motivation can flourish.*

motivational factor increases in specialized work groups or teams within an agency.

Enjoyment, contentment, fulfillment, or plain old-fashioned personal job satisfaction can be powerful internal motivators. These motivators can exist even if the employee dislikes a current assignment but has found one minor aspect of the job personally satisfying. Supervisors would do well to learn what parts of the job their employees enjoy the most and then try to make those work opportunities happen as often as possible.

Competition is another strong internal motivator for some, as it offers both a challenge and the potential for recognition. Even the feeling of value can be an internal motivator. Employees who understand their role in the organization—their purpose—and the importance of their role (regardless of how small) in completing the organization's mission, are more likely to feel motivated about their work.

The more you get to know your employees, the more successful you will be at understanding what motivates them.

The Unmotivated

Leading by example works wonders on those employees who possess the potential to be motivated. However, when it comes to the chronically unmotivated employee, do not beat yourself up for failing to motivate that individual. The failure is theirs, not yours. If they have no wants, desires, or goals that you can help them fulfill, they may be impossible to motivate. They may choose to do only what is required. Even then, they may only do a required task when they decide the consequences for not doing it outweigh the pain of doing what you ask. You can train, retrain, badger, coerce, threaten, discipline, provide endless enticements, and even lead by example, but it will not make a difference to a person who refuses to be motivated.

Work hard to build a positive work environment where most people look forward to coming to work, and where motivation has the chance to flourish. But do so with the understanding that your best efforts may have no influence on motivating the employee who refuses to be motivated.

Some employees should never have been hired. For those employees, it is likely that more management than leadership will be required, and accountability—rather than motivation—will be the answer.

Motivating Yourself

You cannot afford to wait for external motivators to come from your boss. Your motivation must come from within, so you can help create a work environment where motivation for your subordinates can thrive. True motivation is the responsibility of each individual and nowhere is that truer than for you.

Your subordinate's motivation starts with you being motivated. Be a role model and start with yourself first. Do not wait for inspiration to strike. Self-motivation sounds simple enough, but many leaders have the process backwards. It is a mistake to think you must first be motivated to carry out an action.

> *Your subordinate's motivation starts with you being motivated. Be a role model and start with yourself first.*

There are responsibilities you must carry out for which you at first have little motivation. You will find that motivation follows, rather than precedes, action. If you recognize a task that needs to be done, start the task, even if you do not feel motivated. The action itself, particularly the successful completion, or even visible progress towards completion, will develop motivation. That initial motivation results in more progress.

As a supervisor, you need to engage with and provide feedback to employees—some of whom you do not even like. Holding employees accountable is another of your many challenges. Do not wait for a bolt of inspiration to carry out these responsibilities. Nor should you wait until you feel motivated. If you are waiting to be motivated by your own supervisor, know that it may never happen. Rather, initiate the action (any action) that will help you achieve some slight progress towards your goal. The progress itself will provide the motivation for you to continue. Your motivation serves as a positive example for your employees. Motivated supervisors have the drive to achieve, and that drive can be contagious. Your self-motivation can help motivate those you supervise. More importantly, you cannot begin to motivate others until you motivate yourself.

CHAPTER 7

The Leadership Spectrum

In my *Bulletproof Leadership* presentations, I talk about building trust, requiring accountability, communicating clearly, and giving recognition. These basic concepts are not new. Most leaders understand that these concepts have always been the building blocks of effective leadership. But for anyone looking for a one-size-fits-all leadership style to eliminate all your problems, I have some unpleasant news.

Your employees are individuals with varying needs and personalities. You, as an individual leader, differ from other leaders. Your life experiences and personality make it impossible for you to be a carbon copy of other leaders—even other successful leaders. So, there is no perfect style that works for every leader in every situation.

The good news is that in picking the best leadership style for you requires you to look no further than your mirror. Be yourself! Be true to your character and true to who you are as a person. Be yourself unless—and this is important—unless you are a jerk[1]. If you are a jerk and your style of leadership is not working, be less of a jerk. When leaders find that "being yourself" does not seem to be working, it is often because they have allowed themselves to slide to one of the extreme ends of the leadership spectrum.

The Extreme Ends of the Spectrum

Operating from the conflict avoidance end of the leadership spectrum is a problem not just limited to new supervisors. It affects any supervisor who dislikes or avoids conflict so often that their ability to do their job is negatively impacted. They may consider themselves people focused, and a friend of their employees. But the problem is that they avoid conflict and ignore problems that require difficult and sometimes unpopular decisions. They worry excessively about being accused of nitpicking, upsetting employees, and with being liked by everyone. They are sometimes so concerned with what others think of them they do not effectively perform their duties.

At the other extreme are those leaders who operate at the command-and-control end of the leadership spectrum. These supervisors often see themselves as traditional leaders. They can be demanding, hard workers—even workaholics, whose focus is often to get results at all costs.

---

[1] One reader suggested that I use a kinder word than "jerk." But since I chose to avoid cuss words in this book, I thought "jerk" was the perfect word to describe narcissistic, uncaring, or demeaning supervisors.

While many in law enforcement might assume that command-and-control leaders are more common because of the nature of their job, that is not necessarily true. A supervisor may have a certain command presence when dealing with the public, but still be a conflict-avoidance supervisor when dealing with his or her own employees. Today conflict avoidance is one of the most common problems experienced by supervisors, and it is a problem that affects employee morale and motivation.

The Leadership Spectrum

Conflict
Avoidance

Command
& Control

Conflict Avoidance Supervisors

The most significant problem encountered by supervisors operating at the extreme ends of the leadership spectrum is the perceptions held by their employees.

The perceptions that employees share about conflict-avoidance supervisors are that they often ignore problems to avoid conflict. Reliable employees watch and become frustrated as problem employees test the limit of what conflict-avoidance supervisors will allow.

Some employees perceive that such supervisors lack the job knowledge to answer questions, make tough decisions, or hold people accountable. Some believe these supervisors are only concerned with being liked. While it is human nature to want to be liked, a supervisor who makes decisions based primarily on the likability factor is destined for failure.

Employees may perceive a supervisor—who tries to improve his or her likeability by complaining about the organization—as someone who does not care about their organization. A supervisor need not love every aspect of their organization. They do not have to be their organization's most noticeable workaholic or the most visible cheerleader. But effective supervisors are committed to their organization.

Occasionally, conflict-avoidance supervisors join with their chronic complaining subordinates to commiserate about perceived injustices. One supervisor even told me it was his job to join in when his subordinates were complaining because he saw himself as an advocate. Please take note: advocates listen to their subordinates and try to correct legitimate problems. Advocates do not commiserate or complain with subordinates about treatment by supervisors or the organization—especially when such commiseration occurs for the purpose of attempting to improve likability. If you engage in the practice of talking negatively about your supervisors to your subordinates, you have given your subordinates permission to talk about you when you are not present. It is not sound leadership and will contribute to their declining morale and loss of trust and respect for you.

Command-and-Control Supervisors

The employee perception most often generated by command-and-control supervisors is that such supervisors are demeaning, sarcastic, and condescending. They use derogatory humor. They micromanage, are overbearing, and can come across like a bully. Some act this way because they are insecure about their job, so they attempt to show that they are in control. They may be afraid that a subordinate has more knowledge or skill in a certain aspect of the job. While supervisors need basic job competencies to perform their duties, they should understand that knowledge and skill development is something that happens throughout a career. This is true for both supervisors and their subordinates.

You have more skills today than you did one year ago, and you will have even more skills a year from now. Even so, some of your subordinates may have a higher level of skill in certain areas. You should not feel insecure because an employee may have more knowledge or skill than you in a specific area. Supervisors would be more successful if they knew the skills and strengths of their subordinates and utilized those strengths to help accomplish the mission. Besides better serving the organization and its mission, a supervisor who uses their subordinate's full potential helps raise the self-esteem and job satisfaction of that employee.

Some command-and-control supervisors are so hard working and task focused that they come across as aloof. They appear to be stuck-up or disinterested in their subordinates. Sometimes they appear to lack both self-confidence and simple people skills. Hard work and technical skills might have helped a supervisor get promoted. But those attributes alone are not enough to make a supervisor an exemplary leader. Supervisors need people skills. If they are lacking in those skills, they need to be smart enough to know they need to make some personal improvements.

Some command-and-control supervisors come across like they do not care about individuals. Sure, they care about the organization. They will be the first ones to tell you how busy they are and how important they are in the organization's hierarchy. But they appear to know little about their employees or what is important to those employees. As you will see in the remainder of this book, showing that you care about the wellbeing of your employees is critical to your success as a supervisor.

Where do I fit in?

In trying to decide where you should fit in on the leadership spectrum, many supervisors mistakenly assume they should always be smack dab in the middle of the spectrum between conflict avoidance and command-and-control. Nothing could be further from the truth. It is important to understand that operating out of the extreme ends of the spectrum (conflict avoidance or command-and-control) will cause you problems. But some supervisors are a little more laid-back than others because of either their own personalities or because that style works best with the employees they supervise. Such supervisors might find themselves a little left of center on the leadership spectrum.

Other supervisors are a little more direct and to the point in their natural communication style. They may even be more than a little task focused. If they also have decent people skiils and know when to be more direct or more laid-back, depending on the situation, they can be equally effective even though they might find themselves just to the right of center on the spectrum.

Authentic Leadership

There is a large gray area on the spectrum in which exemplary leaders can move back and forth as the situation warrants without reaching either extreme end of the spectrum and all the problems associated with those extremes. I call this large area in the center *authentic leadership*.

The Leadership Spectrum

Conflict Avoidance ← **Authentic Leadership** → Command & Control

Authentic leadership means being true to yourself. It means working within your comfort zone—most of the time. But it also means having the ability to adjust outside of your comfort zone when the situation requires either a more passive or more assertive response.

Your Target Employee Perceptions

The target employee perceptions authentic leaders want to generate is that they are committed to their organization. They do not have to be a workaholic, but they need to show that they believe in and support the organization. A leader can be temporarily (and privately) upset by either the organization or one of his or her bosses and still be committed to the organization.

Authentic leaders also generate an employee perception that they care about employees as individuals. They know their employees. They engage with their employees. They know what is important to their employees both on and off the job. Caring about employees does not mean the supervisor avoids conflict or gives the employees everything they desire. Occasionally, supervisors make corrections or give orders that anger employees. It is a difficult dance to be committed to an organization and show you care about employees at the same time. But it is a dance that authentic leaders make daily.

Authentic leaders are open to employee input and ideas. That does not mean a supervisor must implement every idea. Sometimes employees have outstanding ideas or legitimate concerns that should be addressed, but occasionally, they just want a supervisor to listen.

Authentic leaders recognize exemplary work. Their recognition is not limited to an employee's meritorious achievements. Rather, authentic leaders recognize employee behavior that they like, appreciate, and would like to see repeated. It cannot be over emphasized—what gets recognized, gets repeated.

Finally, authentic leaders hold employees accountable. That does not mean they enjoy disciplining subordinates. It means that they set expectations and hold people accountable to those expectations. Accountability benefits good employees even more than problem employees, because it demonstrates that their supervisor cares enough to pay attention to the behavior and performance of all emoployees.

CHAPTER 8

Self-Awareness

While authentic leadership is a practical concept, it only works if a leader has, and uses, a high degree of self-awareness. Self-awareness is essential for leaders to know when their form of authentic leadership is working or not working. They need to know when it is working to help meet organizational goals and objectives and when it is working to get the best performance from individual employees. They also need to know when it is not working, so they can make corrections.

Authentic leadership is an achievable goal for most executives, managers, and supervisors of every rank. It should not take a degree in leadership or decades of experience to comprehend the benefits of achieving certain target employee perceptions. It should not surprise any leader that they might benefit from their employees perceiving that they are both committed to the organization and care about employees as individuals. Most supervisors know that they should be open to their employees' ideas and input; they should recognize their superb work; and they should hold employees accountable for poor performance or unacceptable behavior. If such target perceptions are—or should be—common knowledge among leaders, why do so many fail in their leadership efforts? Why is it that so many leaders operate from the far and ineffective extremes of the leadership spectrum? The simple answer is: They lack self-awareness.

A high level of self-awareness is essential for effective leadership. It is one of the building blocks of authentic leadership, without which no leader can be successful. You may have worked for, or known, an ineffective manager or supervisor operating at the far extremes of the leadership spectrum. At least some of those so-called leaders had to realize that a steep decline in

> *A high level of self-awareness is essential for effective leadership.*

motivation, morale, and performance was at least partially their fault. At times, their lack of self-awareness caused them to continue their destructive habits costing, not only a loss of employee commitment, but a loss of their job.

Anecdotal Experiences

You may have worked with conflict-avoidance supervisors who did whatever they could to avoid any conflict. Talented employees became discouraged and frustrated when they came to realize their underperforming coworkers were never held accountable for their actions. The morale and performance of even the best workers began to decline. Apathy became normal. Turnovers increased. Some employees transferred off the supervisor's shift, and others sought employment in different organizations. The turnovers may have even included hard-working subordinate supervisors who had reached their wits' end working for a boss who avoided accountability and conflict at all costs. Conflict avoidance supervisors are frequently described by subordinates as a pleasant person, but an ineffective (even clueless) leader. Such supervisors lose the trust of almost everyone they supervise.

You may have worked with command-and-control supervisors whose leadership habits included demeaning employees, micromanaging, being more than a little insecure, and coming across like they just did not care about individuals.

Over several years, one such police chief, by his words and actions, alienated most of his employees, neighboring law enforcement organizations, the media, and many residents in his

> *Failure to recognize when your leadership strategy is not working is a critical (and sometimes career ending) error.*

community. He caused so many problems that the appointing authority ordered a management study that subsequently produced a list of suggested changes. The chief was given three years to implement the suggestions. He refused, saying he knew what was best for the organization. He was forced to retire.

It is important to note that this chief had considerable on-the-job experience. He had also attended numerous leadership seminars and conferences where he collected certificates of attendance to leadership workshops. But he never applied the leadership strategies he had learned. He lacked the self-awareness to understand that his own words and actions caused his downfall.

Being a driven results-focused leader sounds like an admirable trait. Even obsessing about being liked or accommodating employees to avoid conflict seems harmless enough. But both command-and-control and conflict-avoidance leaders can leave a trail of carnage in their wakes. Evidence of that carnage is a loss of employee trust and a decline in their morale, motivation, and commitment. Self-awareness is essential to prevent leaders from engaging in these destructive practices. But self-awareness is not about reflection alone. Sometimes self-awareness comes from the insight gained from others—especially those you supervise. Have the courage to ask this question. *What is it like to work for me?*

Failure to recognize when your leadership strategy is not working is a critical error. Compounding that error by not changing strategies, when needed to become more effective, can cost you your job. The importance of self-awareness in authentic leadership cannot be overstated.

Three Universal Truths

I am often asked if people, especially leaders, can change. I believe the answer is a resounding yes, but that answer comes with a caveat. People can change if they want to change. An evil, narcissistic leader does not become a decent human being and caring leader by accident. A mediocre, ineffective leader does not become a confident and inspiring effective leader just because he or she reads a book or attends a seminar. Leaders can and often do improve their leadership skills by gaining new knowledge. But they must be willing to apply that knowledge.

Although self-awareness is important, even self-awareness alone is not enough. Actual change—real improvement in leadership skills—comes from applying what you learn in formal and informal training opportunities. It comes from learning from your experiences (mistakes, failures, and successes). And it comes from having the desire to change.

Unfortunately, positive change in leadership skills, even by the most well-intentioned leader, will not always produce immediate results. In fact, for a few employees the desired results may never be achieved despite the best efforts of a committed, hard-working leader. Those leaders willing to travel the road to improvement in their own leadership journey should understand the following three universal truths:

1. Any change that you make in your leadership strategy will change your employees' work environment. Any positive change will produce, eventually if not immediately, better performance results and more commitment by most employees.

2. Some employees will be slower to adapt or acknowledge the positive changes you implement than others. Some may be suspicious of your

intentions based on their past experiences. Some may take a more cautious wait-and-see approach, even when the change is in their best interest.

3. Some employees will never adapt to the positive changes you implement. They may view your positive changes as a form of manipulation or further proof of the organization's injustice. The conspiracy theorists may see manipulation even in your most well-meaning leadership efforts.

It is important to understand that most employees will benefit from your efforts to create a positive work environment. But supervisors attempting to make such efforts should not be disheartened by the few disgruntled employees whose commitment, job satisfaction, or morale seems impossible to improve—even by the best of leaders. Do not allow a few such employees to poison your will or desire to change how you lead your employees.

CHAPTER 9

Role Models

Can you remember a supervisor you thought was an excellent leadership role model? You may not always remember the exact leadership principles that supervisor applied, but you probably remember how the supervisor made you feel. It is common to recall supervisors who made you feel motivated, inspired, and valued. You can recall those supervisors who mentored you, from whom you learned, and who made it enjoyable to come to work. Even if you might be unsure about what it takes to become an effective supervisor, you know it is important to make subordinates feel like that supervisor made you feel.

Coincidently, you may have learned just as much about leadership from a bad role model. If nothing else, you learned not to be like that person, or at least not to make your employees feel like that supervisor made you feel.

The Role Model Exercise

One of the exercises I have done many times in my seminars is to ask attendees to think back on their most influential supervisor regardless of whether they perceived that person to be an excellent or a terrible leader. I then divide the class into two groups—good and bad role model examples. The attendees are usually equally divided.

Next, I ask them to give me the single trait commonly shown by their role model choice. Those in the bad role model group tell me of supervisors who were demeaning, lazy, bullies, and liars. They tell me about supervisors who lacked confidence or had integrity issues. They tell me about supervisors who were micromanagers, and others who were seldom seen. What they learned most from such supervisors was not to be like that bad role model.

Those in the good role model group tell of supervisors who led by example, had integrity, were enthusiastic, and cared about employees. They tell of supervisors who were confident without being arrogant, who held people accountable, and who made sure employees knew what to expect so no one had to guess.

The Issue of Trust

When the two groups are finished talking about the traits of their good and bad role models, I ask each group if they trusted the supervisor they are describing. For those in the bad role model group, the answer is always a resounding no. I have done this exercise hundreds of times and the results are always the same. Regardless of the many reasons a subordinate might decide their supervisor was a bad role model, the result is that the subordinate does not trust that supervisor. I then ask this follow-up question: Did you feel comfortable talking to that supervisor about problems on or off the job, questions, concerns, or new ideas? The answer is always the same. If they do not trust the supervisor, they will go out of their way to avoid communicating with that person for any reason. In some cases, that means finding the answer elsewhere. In other cases, it means not reporting potential problems and mistakes. Even new ideas stay hidden from that supervisor.

When I ask the same questions to those in the good role model group, the answer is always that they trust that supervisor. There can be 100 different reasons why people think their supervisor was an effective leader; but the results are always the same. If they believe the supervisor was a good role model, they trust that supervisor. When I ask if they felt comfortable talking to that supervisor, the answer is always, "Of course." They feel comfortable going to such supervisors with questions, ideas, concerns, problems, even with mistakes they have made. They feel comfortable because they know they will be listened to and not be demeaned.

A Lack of Trust

A lack of trust is the number one reason for communication failures. Communication failures between supervisors and subordinates not only stagnates growth, but can cause serious problems for the supervisor, the subordinate, and the organization. The potential for negative consequences is real. The exercise I described has demonstrated over and over that in building trust, a supervisor's actions have consequences.

If there is no trust, there is little or no communication. If there is no communication, there is no early warning that the supervisor is making critical errors in his or her approach to leadership. If there is no early warning, and if the supervisor's self-awareness is not working as it should, there is no chance for correction. Not every supervisor fails because of intentional poor leadership choices. Some fail because they had no idea that they were engaging in ineffective leadership practices and their subordinates did not trust them enough to provide any early warning. If there is no correction in the poor leadership choices being made, the supervisor will lose all commitment from his or her subordinates. Such a downward spiral can cause a ruined reputation; and, occasionally, it can cost a supervisor his or her job.

> It is your responsibility to create a work environment where subordinates feel comfortable talking to you about any issue.

One participant in the exercise told me, "It's not my job to tell my supervisor he's screwing up. It's not my responsibility." He was right. It was not his job or his responsibility to tell his supervisor he was doing something wrong, killing employee morale, or that his career was going down in flames. Rather, it was his supervisor's responsibility to create a work environment where subordinates felt comfortable talking to him about those problems. It is your responsibility to create a work environment where your employees feel comfortable communicating with you for any reason.

CHAPTER 10

Building Trust

Building trust is like putting money in a savings account. You make deposits when you can to help build your future and to act as a safeguard in times of crisis. When you make withdrawals, your account balance diminishes. If you continue to make withdrawals without making deposits, you will completely empty your account. The trust that exists between you and your employees is like that savings account. You make deposits by your words and actions that earn employee trust. You make withdrawals by words and actions that lose their trust. Trust is seldom given as a gift; it must be earned. Most supervisors work hard to try to earn trust, but many are unaware of how easily it can be lost.

Trust Withdrawals

Imagine having a difficult, but much-needed, discussion with a subordinate about inappropriate behavior. Assume the correction you gave was professional and justified. Even though your words might be correct for the situation, the employee still feels picked on or demeaned. The result is the employee loses a little trust in you at that moment.

It may seem unfair to lose trust when you make a conscious decision and you know you are doing what is right. Understand that every supervisor will occasionally make a tough decision likely to anger a subordinate, resulting in at least a little loss of trust. At least if you are aware of what you did, you can work on rebuilding trust. Unfortunately, from time to time, circumstances might occur that result in a loss of trust where you are not even aware that a withdrawal occurred, much less why it occurred.

Simple misunderstandings, rumors, or misperceptions happen almost daily. Your words, actions, and omissions, and even your humor, can all contribute to a loss of trust. Imagine one of your employees waving to you to say hello, but you failed to notice the employee. That perceived slight, even if unintentional, can cause a loss of trust.

> *Trust withdrawals happen every day. Find ways to make regular deposits in your trust account.*

If you combine the withdrawals, caused by your conscious (and correct) decisions, with the withdrawals you were unaware you caused, you have the potential for a serious loss of trust. The only way to counter those withdrawals is to make frequent deposits. Be proactive. Make deposits to build trust so that any intentional or unintentional withdrawal does not drain your trust account. Look for ways to make deposits that will earn trust. To help you remember this strategy, think of the word **D.E.P.O.S.I.T.S.**

D—Deem it a Deposit

Good intentions do not equal a deposit. For your words or actions to be a trust deposit, the employee must deem it to be a deposit. While a supervisor's best intentions, combined with actual effort, might deserve extra points (and doing the right thing is never a waste of time) real deposits occur when the employee feels trust has been earned.

Take for example, the often-quoted phrase "Lead by example." For some supervisors, that means getting out of the office and just being seen by their employees. To others, it means pitching in to do the actual work. A subordinate might appreciate either action, find one or both meaningless, or they might even view either as a trust withdrawal. It is not so much about the supervisor's words or actions as it is about the subordinate's perception.

> Good intentions are not enough. Real deposits only happen if your words or actions are deemed a deposit by your employees.

Plus, that perception may be different for individual employees. There is no need to decide in advance that a word or action is, or is not, a trust-building moment. It is important, however, not to make assumptions. Just because you consider something a deposit does not mean all your employees consider your words or actions a deposit.

Deposits can take many forms. A supervisor who leaves the office and engages employees in conversations about "the job," or about their families or their hobbies has an opportunity to build trust. However, employees have different interests. So, supervisors who know their employees well enough to have meaningful conversations about topics that interest employees will have the best chance of earning and building employee trust.

Even professional development can be a trust-building opportunity. Some employees view those who provide career guidance as trusted mentors. While supervisors are not always able to provide formal professional development opportunities, when they can provide or suggest opportunities in line with the interests and goals of the subordinate, they have a unique opportunity to build trust. It is imperative for supervisors to remember that employees are individuals. Career guidance or professional development that builds trust for one employee could be meaningless to another employee with different career goals.

E—Easy Going

Deposits rarely take place in formal meetings, performance evaluations, reprimand situations, or during most meetings in your office. Even when you tell an employee their performance evaluation is above average, there is always the chance for a little anxiety in any formal situation. The higher the potential for anxiety or uncertainty, the less likelihood there is to build trust. The more informal or casual an encounter or conversation is with the subordinate, the greater the chance of building trust.

P—Personal Integrity

Personal integrity is the most important component needed for trust building. Any supervisor perceived by a subordinate to lack personal integrity may find it impossible to build trust. If there is no integrity, there will be no trust. Here are a few suggestions to guide supervisors in their efforts to maintain their own personal integrity.

> *If you are perceived by your subordinates to lack personal integrity, you may find it impossible to build trust.*

- **Be a role model.** Personal integrity for a supervisor can take many forms. The easiest place to start is by being a trustworthy role model. Set the example—lead by example. Do not be a rule breaker or a rule bender. Do not expect others to follow rules you ignore. Do not allow others to break or bend rules, hoping they will complain less if you bend the rules. Personal integrity has nothing to do with being a by-the-book rules and regulations zealot, and everything to do with accountability, responsibility, and trust.

- **Never lie.** Lie to an employee and you will empty your trust account. And it will be a long time before they trust you again. If you are asked a question and are unsure of an answer, do not make something up that might later be perceived to be a lie. Let subordinates know you will try to find the correct answer. If the answer is a subject that is confidential, let the subordinates know you are not free to discuss the matter.

- **Keep your promises.** Supervisors should generally avoid making promises. But if you make a promise, do your best to keep it. Even telling a subordinate you will meet them at a certain place and time and then forgetting to do so will be seen as a broken promise by some subordinates. If you break a promise because you had no choice, or because of something you forgot, apologize and work to rebuild trust.

- **Keep confidences.** There are times when it is necessary to report inappropriate or unlawful behavior to your supervisor. But there are times when you may be asked to keep something in confidence. Employee personal problems, medical problems, or someone seeking career advice are just a few examples. Sharing personal information given to you in confidence is a sure way to lose a subordinate's trust—and the trust of every other employee who hears about your lack of integrity.

- **Do not gossip.** Gossip is derogatory comments or character assassination against coworkers who are not present to defend themselves. It does not matter if the gossip is true, or if you agree with the gossip. Gossip is the sharing of hurtful information for no other purpose than spite. If you take part in the gossip or allow it to happen, you will be deemed a gossiper and will lose the trust of your subordinates. You may be unable to cure gossip throughout your entire organization, but you can clarify that it is an unacceptable behavior you will not tolerate. Working hard to make all employees know that you want everyone under your supervision treated with dignity and respect will not only minimize gossip, it will help build trust.

- **Do not use derogatory or demeaning humor.**
Humor can often make the job more enjoyable and can reduce both stress and boredom. Unfortunately, humor can have a dark side. Derogatory or demeaning humor from a supervisor, directed at a subordinate, can have serious consequences. Inappropriate humor can even result in lawsuits against supervisors or their organizations. At the very least, it can cause a loss of trust between the supervisor and the targeted subordinate.
These cautionary words about derogatory humor do not mean to imply that good-natured banter between those of the same rank who willingly engage with each other is always inappropriate. But problems arise when offensive banter is directed at a subordinate. Because of the perceived power

difference, the subordinate may not feel he or she can respond in kind, and the banter can make the employee feel they are being bullied by a supervisor.

A subordinate targeted by derogatory humor may not complain because of embarrassment. Do not view their silence as appreciation for being the target of a supervisor's joke. Employees who feel demeaned by a supervisor (even through the use of humor) might remain silent, but still come to distrust that supervisor.

O—Outside Your Office

An open-door policy is often thought to be an essential element of trust building. But while the concept can build trust, it is not without potential problems.

Employees may use an open-door policy to circumvent an established chain of command. In doing so, they avoid telling their immediate supervisor about a problem that might have been more appropriately handled by that supervisor. If you want subordinates to adhere to a formal chain of command, you will need to set ground rules so subordinates know what situations you will listen to and what situations will be referred back to a subordinate supervisor. Open-door policies can work, but certain job-related problems should first be addressed by or sent back to the employee's immediate supervisor.

Open-door policies have the potential to cause other problems as well. Some employees might feel uncomfortable going to your office to talk about anything. Some might be concerned about peer pressure. They might even enjoy conversing with you about a hobby you both have in common, but are hesitant to have that conversation in your office out of fear that coworkers might accuse them of being a suck-up or of ratting on fellow employees.

You might even encounter an employee who enjoys going to your office to have long conversations. Chronic complainers probably enjoy going to your office. Manipulative employees also enjoy going to your office. They know that an extra-long conversation with you about your favorite pastime might temporarily delay them from returning to their work. Have conversations, but do not allow yourself to be the victim of manipulation. Redirect and refocus chronic complainers and manipulative employees and politely end the conversation at an appropriate time, so they can get back to their duties.

If you want to build trust through employee encounters and casual conversations, you will be more successful if you go to their workspace. Employees always feel most comfortable in their own work area. Have conversations at those locations.

Going to them has many advantages. First, it shows you care enough to make a conscious effort to go engage them personally. Second, going to them takes away any potential stigma the employee might feel regarding going to you in your office. Whether it be their workspace or a more casual location, conversations where they feel comfortable are likely to build more trust than formal settings.

One word of caution regarding a time-tested strategy called "management by walking around" or MBWA. True engagement with employees and real trust deposits require more than just walking around adding steps to your fitness tracker. It requires more than just being seen or giving your subordinates an insincere thumbs-up signal so you can fool yourself that you engaged with your employees.

> *MBWA is not about putting steps on your fitness tracker. It means regularly engaging with and conversing with all your employees.*

Engagement means that in addition to going to them and showing your face, that you have a conversation with the employee. MBWA is not just about walking. It is about having real trust-building supervisor-employee engagement.

S—Special Situations

Special situations are the milestones or important events that occur in the lives of your employees. A special situation is any situation or circumstance that influences how an employee feels at work. The reason special situations are so important is that how an employee feels at work often affects the employee's morale, motivation, and performance. Special situations are memorable moments (both pleasant and unpleasant) that influence how the employee feels. A supervisor who is alert enough to notice an employee's special situation is in a unique position to offer congratulations, condolences, or just a few kind words when they are needed most. It is an opportunity to show employees you care enough about their wellbeing to be aware of what is going on in their lives. Your interaction may be as memorable to the employee as the situation.

There are certain events in the lives of employees that most would consider positive and memorable, including, but not limited to, weddings, milestone anniversaries, the birth of a child, christenings, graduations, or major achievements by the employee or an employee's family member. If the situation or event is important to your employee, it should be important to you.

It is equally important to take notice of tragic, or unpleasant memorable events and to offer condolences when appropriate, empathy, or just a willingness to listen. Such circumstances include the death or serious injury, or sickness of an employee's family member. On occasion, an employee may need a card or a few words of compassion.

It does not matter if an employee's special situation seems trivial to you. It only matters that the situation is important to the employee and that you take notice.

At other times, attending a wake or funeral, or a hospital visit would be appropriate. Employees have long memories about supervisors who show they care by word and action during times of personal crisis. They have even longer memories about supervisors who were unseen, unheard, or who made callous comments during these times.

With unpleasant special situations, not all those memorable occurrences will, at first, seem like they are worthy of your special attention. But know that an employee whose teenage daughter is involved in a minor no-injury traffic accident, or whose old Labrador Retriever died that day, is an employee who is having a dreadful day. It does not matter if the situation seems trivial to you. It only matters that the situation is important to the employee.

Stay alert for special situations, both positive and negative, that arise in the lives of your employees. Be present when appropriate. Offer congratulations, condolences, and compassion. Say a few kind words or just listen when they need an empathetic ear. If you ignore or forget a special situation, know that your employee will not ignore or forget your absence or omissions.

I—Individually

Trust-building efforts are most effective—and the results most obvious—when efforts are focused on individual employees rather than groups. Building trust happens one person at a time. Each employee is different and has different needs and desires. They also have different perceptions about both the level of trust that exists and the trust-building efforts of their supervisors. Some employees need continuous feedback to feel appreciated by their supervisor. Other employees receiving the same level of feedback might feel micromanaged by what they perceive as excessive feedback.

Some employees feel their supervisor cares about them because the supervisor talks about their job performance and professional development. Other employees feel appreciated because a supervisor asks about the health of the employee's elderly parents. Some employees trust their supervisor because that supervisor allows them to do their jobs without micromanagement and gives employees additional responsibilities. And some employees believe a supervisor cares about them because the supervisor has casual conversations with them about their hobbies. Pick any ten employees, and you might need ten unique approaches to successfully build trust in those individuals.

T - Thoughtfulness

Thoughtfulness is not rocket science. It should be common sense, or at least common decency. Thoughtfulness is about treating people with dignity and respect—just like you would like to be treated. It is about showing kindness, compassion, and empathy. And the best news is that there is no heavy lifting required. Just look around for opportunities to show a little thoughtfulness.

There is no need to wait for a major achievement or milestone. Any employee's birthday, an employee buying a new car, an employee going or coming back from vacation, an employee returning to work after being out sick, or an employee's family getting a new puppy—all may seem like minor occurrences to you. On the contrary, they are all important to the employee. No major celebration is required in these situations, but a few thoughtful words in casual conversation may equal a major trust deposit.

Occasionally, supervisors hear information about an employee from their coworkers. Do not dismiss such information as being useless hearsay. Please note that I am not talking about spiteful information, rumors or gossip which should not be tolerated. I am referring to both the pleasant and unpleasant things that occur in the lives of your employees that you do not always hear about firsthand. It would be great if all your subordinates told you about situations affecting how they feel at work directly. Unfortunately, many employees do not want to burden their supervisors with such personal information. Hearing it from coworkers may give you the opportunity to respond with congratulations, compassion, or some other caring and appropriate response. Just make sure you are not responding to (or tolerating) rumors or gossip.

> A little kindness can equal a big trust deposit. A little unkindness will equal a major withdrawal.

News such as an employee's daughter scoring the winning point at a high school basketball game; a son making the National Honor Society; a spouse injured in a fall; or an elderly mother transported by ambulance to the hospital, are all situations where a caring supervisor should respond appropriately. Whether you learn about such circumstances firsthand from the employee or you overhear coworkers discussing the situation (in a manner that is not spiteful, rumor or gossip) does not matter. What matters is your response.

Note, too, that it only takes a little unkindness to result in a major trust withdrawal. Any unkind word, or sarcastic or demeaning comment that you thought was funny can result in a significant loss of trust. Something as simple as omitting or forgetting to congratulate or console an employee in a circumstance—where it would have been the right thing to do—will cause a loss of trust. Forgetting to attend an important event, such as the funeral of an employee's immediate family member, can cause a serious loss of trust. Likewise, any lie or perceived lie, a broken promise, gossiping about an employee, or any other acts or omissions considered by the employee to be demeaning, thoughtless, or unkind will cause a loss of trust that the supervisor will find hard to rebuild.

S - Sorry

Occasionally, supervisors make mistakes with employees that result in a loss of trust. They forget things. They think they are being funny, but their comments are perceived as demeaning. They break promises. They say things that might occur. And then when they fail to happen, their words are perceived as a lie. Supervisors occasionally get angry at employees and are carried away by emotions and may say things to coworkers that they later regret. There are many circumstances in which a supervisor meant to do the right thing, but failed, resulting in a major loss of trust. Attempts to rebuild that trust start with a sincere apology.

A sincere apology can help to minimize the damage you caused when you made a trust withdrawal. At times, a sincere apology may even build a little trust. But not all apologies are created equal. If the apology is not sincere, it can do more harm than good. If a supervisor continually makes derogatory comments, and after each such comment the supervisor halfheartedly apologizes—only when he or she learns that the employee is upset—the apology will be meaningless. Never be afraid to offer a sincere apology when you are wrong or when your words, actions, or omissions resulted in a loss of trust.

A final thought on building and earning trust. A supervisor's trust-building efforts must be ongoing—every day. There are so many situations, words, acts, and omissions that result in a loss of trust, that supervisors must be ever vigilant for trust-building opportunities. If you ever think you have built enough trust and can take a break from your trust building efforts, please consider *The Rent Axiom*.

The Rent Axiom

> *Trust is never owned.*
> *It is only rented,*
> *and the rent is due every single day!*

CHAPTER 11

Accountability

Accountability is a word often misunderstood and occasionally feared. Too many supervisors believe accountability is all about nitpicking, discipline, and punishment. And some see their job as protecting their subordinates from accountability.

Why Accountability Matters

Why does accountability matter? It matters because it shows you care enough about your employees to pay attention to their performance. Accountability matters because it shows that your expectations are important. And accountability matters because it shows that your employee's competent work matters, and that mediocre or unacceptable work and behavior will not be tolerated. Accountability is not about getting employees in trouble. It is about helping them meet your expectations.

Many employees, including many supervisors, view accountability as harsh, unsympathetic, and unfair treatment by either the organization or by a by-the-book supervisor. This mistaken belief is often reinforced by supervisors who fail to understand the purpose of accountability and use it like a bludgeon on employees who make them angry. Command-and-control supervisors, for example, at times, use accountability to demean or embarrass employees. They enjoy the discovery of every *gotcha* moment. Such supervisors often rule by fear, vindictiveness, and the power of their rank or position. Their misuse of accountability causes other supervisors to feel they need to protect their subordinates.

Just as supervisors, who use accountability like a hammer, hurt morale and performance, those supervisors who try to protect their subordinates, by failing to hold anyone accountable, also hurt morale and performance. Competent employees rarely trust or respect supervisors who allow troublesome, incompetent, or lazy employees to continue seemingly unnoticed. Talented employees want their capable work recognized and want unacceptable performance appropriately managed.

Discipline

The formal progressive discipline process is part of the rules and regulations or policies and procedures of almost every organization. The process dictates consequences for certain behaviors. Accountability, in of itself, is not discipline. Discipline is not required every time an employee makes a mistake or cannot meet a supervisor's expectation. There is a time and a place for discipline, but most encounters between a supervisor and a subordinate who needs correction or improvement, do not require discipline.

Punishment

Punishment is the act of imposing a penalty for an offense. While punishment can include termination, many problem employees receive punishment just short of termination. Unfortunately, some of those punished employees remain bitter and angry for the rest of their careers. Like discipline, there is a time and place for punishment, including termination. But in many cases, accountability used appropriately might reduce the need to impose punishment.

So why is discipline and punishment (or an organization's traditional progressive discipline process) so ineffective at correcting problems? The diagram on the next page might help explain the problem. This is a typical supervisory response to an observed problem and why traditional disciplinary efforts so often fail.

The Progressive Discipline Cycle

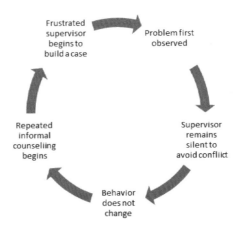

Frustrated supervisor begins to build a case

Problem first observed

Supervisor remains silent to avoid confliict

Repeated informal counseliing begins

Behavior does not change

The Progressive Discipline Cycle

Step 1: The problem behavior, mistake, or poor performance is first observed.

Step 2: The supervisor takes little or no action. Supervisors do not want to be accused of nitpicking or of making a big issue out of a minor behavior or performance problem.

Step 3: The inappropriate behavior or poor performance does not change. Silence is a reward for poor behavior, causing it to be repeated.

Step 4: As the supervisor's frustration increases with the employee's failure to improve, the supervisor engages in repeated "counseling," which at this late stage may have little effect.

Step 5: The supervisor becomes frustrated and angry with the employee (and at his or her own inability to influence the employee) and begins to build a formal case for discipline or punishment, up to and including termination. At this stage, the supervisor's mindset has changed from wanting to help to "we need to document everything" to get rid of the problem employee (either by transfer or termination).

Too often, supervisors observe repeated mistakes by a single employee and wonder why future mistakes are not corrected by their repeated causal conversations with that employee. And too often, a series of mistakes, or unacceptable behaviors continue over months or years, yet no one recognizes the potential risk to the organization.

> *Lawyers focus on fixing problems after they occur. Real risk managers focus on addressing problems before they occur.*
> —Gordon Graham

Retired California Highway Patrol supervisor and risk management expert Gordon Graham says that, "Risk management is the process of looking into the future (short or long term), asking what can go wrong and then doing something to prevent it from going wrong." The trends that supervisors see or should see in their employees should serve as a crystal ball to help them predict future potential problems and provide a pathway for correction.

Employees with chronic problems, or those who commit repeated mistakes, or who engage in repeated unacceptable behavior are exhibiting predictable future behavior. Those situations require a supervisor with the courage to interrupt that trend to prevent a future problem from occurring. As Gordon has often said, "Lawyers focus on fixing problems *after* they occur. Real risk managers focus on addressing problems *before* they occur." Supervisors at all levels of their organization need to become *real* risk managers.

The diagram that follows shows an entirely different type of cycle and supervisory response. Consider how this might be more effective than the traditional response to an employee problem and help you become a *real* risk manager.

The Accountability Cycle

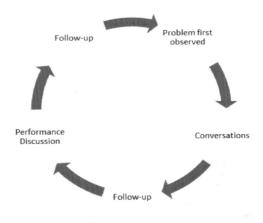

Follow-up

Problem first observed

Performance Discussion

Conversations

Follow-up

The Accountability Cycle

Step 1: The problem behavior, mistake or poor performance is first observed.

Step 2: The supervisor has an informal conversation with the employee about his or her concerns or observations. Most supervisors do this already but wait too long to have that first conversation. Have the conversation when you first observe the issue.

Step 3: Follow-up is important. If you get the results you want, let the employee know you appreciate the change. If there is no improvement, decide if more conversations are appropriate or more formal steps should be taken.

Step 4: For problems that cannot be corrected by informal conversations, have a performance discussion. Performance discussions are formal discussions that clearly state the supervisor's observations and expectations and ask the employee for commitment to meet those expectations.

Step 5: Follow-up after performance discussions are crucial. Give recognition for improvement and initiate consequences for failure or refusal to improve.

Conversations. Initiate conversations when the problem is first observed, but do not have repeated unproductive conversations. If you do not get the results you want, move on to performance discussions.

Performance Discussions. Performance discussions are more formal than conversations. There is no misunderstanding about the nature of a performance discussion. Such discussions assertively and directly (but with professionalism) explain the observed problem and the supervisor's expectations. Most importantly, such discussions end by the supervisor asking for the employee's commitment to correct the problem.

Follow-up. Follow-up is essential at every stage of the process. Follow-up includes continuous feedback, and sometimes even documentation. Follow-up also includes giving recognition for correcting the problem, or consequences for failure or refusal to improve.

Performance

Accountability is not about nitpicking, it is not about discipline, and it is not about punishment. Holding employees accountable is about one thing and one thing only: future performance. It is imperative that supervisors hold employees accountable for their behaviors and their performance so that future behavior and performance can be improved. Accountability should never be used by a supervisor to embarrass or demean a subordinate. Setting clear expectations, providing guidance to help employees meet those expectations, and pointing out and correcting mistakes so they are not repeated is an essential supervisory function.

Why is it so important to correct mistakes, inappropriate behavior, and poor performance right at the beginning? Consider something I call *The Performance Lesson*.

The Performance Lesson

Practice doesn't make perfect.
Practice makes permanent!

Permanent Behaviors

If you ignore mistakes and inappropriate behavior and allow mediocre or substandard performance to continue, you are telling your employees that such behavior is acceptable. What starts out as a minor issue evolves into a habit and eventually becomes a permanent behavior—the new norm. Stop complaining about bad behavior you are willing to tolerate. But do not be surprised when predictable behavior leads to consequences you should have seen coming. Silence is a reward for unacceptable behavior, causing it to be repeated!

Some supervisors who read this may think I am suggesting terminating all problem employees. I am not suggesting you weed out employees; I am suggesting you weed out inappropriate behavior. You want employees to stay, but they need to meet the organization's (and your) performance expectations. But let us not kid ourselves. Not everyone is cut out for a career in law enforcement. Some employees should have been weeded out in the hiring process. You do your community, your organization, your subordinates, and yourself a terrible disservice by tolerating the behavior of a problem employee. You owe it to those you supervise, and those you serve, to hold employees accountable to reasonable and clearly stated expectations.

Nitpicking

Some readers may think all this talk about accountability sounds like nitpicking. Let us examine for a moment what is and is not nitpicking. Nitpicking is being excessively concerned with or critical of <u>inconsequential</u> details. I have underlined the word "inconsequential" for a reason. If a behavior that bothers you has no consequences—it does not violate a rule or policy, it does not offend others, hurt morale or performance, put people at risk, or contribute to a toxic work environment, maybe the issue is more your personal pet peeve than an inappropriate behavior.

> *Nitpicking is being excessively concerned with or critical of <u>inconsequential</u> details.*
>
> *Correcting unacceptable behavior that has predictable consequences is not nitpicking. It's called leadership!*

If you review a police report from a subordinate and it has all the necessary content, the grammar and spelling are acceptable, it meets or exceeds the expected standards, and it will not embarrass the employee or the organization if read later in court, it is probably an acceptable report. If you conclude, however, that the report is not written as well as if you wrote it and send it back to be rewritten, you might be doing a little nitpicking. Occasionally, supervisors have personal pet peeves—they expect employees to do things exactly as they did them—and those pet peeves can feel like nitpicking to employees. Supervisors should be looking for excellence, not their personal view of perfection. Make sure your excessively critical comments are not focused on inconsequential details.

Now if the report we discussed lacks basic information, or has so many spelling mistakes that it would embarrass the employee if the report was read in court, it would not be nitpicking to send it back to the employee for correction. Such a review and return to the employee of a report with critical errors and mistakes is a perfect example of accountability.

Never Walk Past a Mistake

Never walk past (or ignore) a mistake that has consequences. It is not nitpicking to correct even minor mistakes—if allowing those mistakes will have consequences. Correcting mistakes is not nitpicking—it is early intervention, and early intervention minimizes the need for formal discipline. Early intervention of unacceptable behavior can prevent predictable negative consequences. Plus, early intervention is an opportunity to train future leaders on what is acceptable and unacceptable behavior and performance.

Where do I start?
The concept of accountability, early intervention, and risk management is new to many supervisors. Those supervisors often ask where they should start.

> **Start by stopping the inappropriate, unprofessional (morale killing) behavior that you <u>observe</u>!**

I am not suggesting that supervisors, who for years have ignored problems, suddenly come to work one morning and decide they can fix every wayward behavior. I suggest starting with those problems that are most obvious and causing the most damage to employee morale and performance. Stop worrying about what other supervisors on other shifts are doing and focus on what is best for your subordinates. Examine the behaviors that bother you the most. If it bothers you and affects employee morale or puts people at risk, then it affects performance. If it affects performance, it deserves your feedback!

CHAPTER 12

The Importance of Feedback

Feedback is the lifeblood of your organization and it is, or should be, an essential job function for all supervisors. Feedback to your subordinates should be ongoing and continuous throughout the year. Sadly, there are supervisors who believe that feedback provided once a year during a performance evaluation is sufficient. In organizations without performance evaluations, supervisors often admit that the only feedback they provide is if an award-worthy event occurs, or if an employee makes enough mistakes to deserve the supervisor's verbal wrath. Obviously, there is a lot of behavior that takes place between award-worthy praise and well-deserved criticism.

Why it is important

Continuous feedback helps maintain accountability. The more you keep employees informed on how they are doing, the more likely they will meet your expectations. Most employees hold themselves accountable, and thankfully, most want to do a decent job. Supervisors who provide ongoing feedback are likely to find their accountability efforts made easier. By giving employees the feedback that they need, you help them achieve the performance level that you desire.

Continuous feedback is not just about criticism—constructive or otherwise. Feedback also recognizes employees for exemplary work. Some supervisors believe that if employees are not doing something meritorious or award-worthy, then no recognition is deserved. But even minor improvements should be recognized. If a supervisor is pleased with the observed improvement (even if it is not award-worthy) then providing feedback on that improvement is likely to get the behavior repeated.

Do Not Make Them Guess

Continuous feedback helps keep employees from having to guess how their supervisor perceives they are performing. One of the most significant causes of anxiety in the performance evaluation process is that employees rarely know what score they will receive. This problem is compounded because it is human nature for employees to believe they are doing an excellent job. In fact, an employee is likely to believe that they are working harder and doing a better job than they are really doing. In the absence of feedback throughout the evaluation period, supervisor and subordinate perceptions regarding job performance are likely to differ significantly. More than a few subordinates have been surprised—to the

> *Give feedback so employees don't have to guess how you think they are doing.*

point of anger—by their supervisor's candid performance evaluation. The solution is more feedback prior to the performance evaluation.

Your Expectations

Feedback is essential for removing the guesswork for employees regarding your perceptions. Feedback also provides supervisors with an opportunity to give their employees their clearly stated performance expectations. Employees may know their organization's rules and regulations or policies, but supervisor expectations can differ from shift to shift, or even from supervisor to supervisor. Expectations have nothing to do with quotas, enforcement metrics, or computer statistics. Expectations have everything to do with accountability, feedback, and what individual supervisors expect from their employees. Listed below are just a few examples of expectations from an immediate supervisor to a subordinate.

> *Expectations may differ from supervisor to supervisor. Your employees deserve to know your expectations.*

- *I expect shift members to treat each other with dignity and respect. I will not engage in or tolerate gossip. That means do not make derogatory comments about coworkers who are not present to defend themselves.*

- *I expect you to be accountable for your own behavior and actions. We all make mistakes and learning from those mistakes helps us learn that failure doesn't have to be fatal. If you make a mistake, own up to it, do your best to fix it, and then move on. Do not play The Blame Game.*

- *Treat your coworkers as you would like to be treated.*

- *If you encounter issues on or off the job that impact either your wellbeing or your ability to perform to your usual high standards, please let me know.*

- *I will meet with you both formerly and informally throughout the year to provide you with ongoing feedback regarding my perceptions on your work performance. I never want you to have to guess how I think you are doing.*

- *I expect you to be on time for work with a professional appearance, properly attired, and ready to begin work at the designated time. Have a good work ethic.*

- *I expect that if you have an unforeseen circumstance and you are going to be late for work that you call me and let me know you will be late.*

- *I expect you to be professional in the workplace with your dress, your demeanor, and your conversation.*

- *I expect you to know the Department's rules of conduct and abide by them.*

- *I expect you to be a team player. This means both supporting your coworkers and knowing that they will support you—to their face and behind their back. If your coworker needs help (even for routine non-emergency tasks) don't wait to be asked or told to give assistance.*

- *I expect you to contribute to creating a work environment where people enjoy coming to work.*

- *I expect open, honest, and ongoing communication from you. Be innovative! I want to hear your ideas and opinions. If you see a problem, let me know. If you see a problem and have a solution, that's even better.*

- *I expect you to keep me aware of any problems you encounter on the shift with coworkers, the public, a particular case, or your workload (whether too much or too little).*

- *I expect that you will have some days that are better or worse than others. While I don't expect a positive and enthusiastic attitude every moment (although that would be nice), I do expect a professional attitude and, more importantly, professional behavior at all times.*

- *I expect that you will not engage in inappropriate behavior, excessive force, or criminal activity yourself, and that you will not tolerate such behavior on the part of any other employee, regardless of their rank, position, or seniority.*

- *I expect that if you are ever confronted with a situation where you witness or are asked to condone inappropriate behavior, excessive force, or criminal activity, that you immediately intervene to stop that behavior when possible, and report that behavior to me regardless of the rank, position, or seniority of the involved employee.*

- *I expect you to meet my clearly stated expectations (both written and verbal) whenever you work under my supervision **regardless of whether such expectations are required or even discussed on other shifts or from other supervisors**.*

CHAPTER 13

Behaviors not Attitudes

There is little debate that an employee's poor attitude can be aggravating for any supervisor. Poor attitudes hurt morale and can spread like a disease infecting even your best employees. The difficulty facing supervisors, however, is that attitudes are difficult to manage and impossible to control. Attitudes are a feeling that an employee has about someone or something. Feelings are subjective, not always visible, and not always caused by the workplace or factors under control of the supervisor.

Potential Causes of Attitudes

There are four primary causes of attitude problems.

- **History.** The employee may have had a problem, a disappointment, or encountered a perceived injustice. The issue could even involve a supervisor no longer working for the organization. Bitter employees have long memories.

- **Personal issues.** Personal issues have a significant influence on employee attitudes, even when the situation has nothing to do with the job. Employees may encounter financial problems, relationship problems, divorce, medical, drug and alcohol problems, or other non-job-related issues that affect their attitude. Organizations can offer employee assistance when it is appropriate and supervisors should be understanding about such problems, but neither may cure all attitude problems caused by personal issues.

- **Personality issues.** Some employees seem to thrive on negativity. Supervisors should understand that employees could pass a pre-employment psychological screening and still have personality issues that come across as a poor attitude. Psychiatrists and psychologists have little luck in changing problem personalities. Supervisors should not expect that they will be any more successful.

- **Lack of job satisfaction.** Lack of job satisfaction is a major attitude influencer, especially for employees who have been on the job for several years. Some employees decide that the job is just not as exciting or as fun as they thought it would be when they started. They may be disappointed in their current assignment or inability to receive a desired promotion. Supervisors cannot fix all job satisfaction issues, but have the opportunity, occasionally, to improve job satisfaction. Improvement starts with asking the employee what they like best about their current job. If there is some minor aspect of the job they like, or some achievable goal that they wish to pursue, the supervisor may be able to help. Some employees have had a change in attitude just by attending a training program that allowed them to develop a specialty or expertise in one area. Other employees have been able to change their attitude because a supervisor

> *People enjoy doing things in which they excel. To improve job satisfaction, help your employees recognize those things and focus their efforts there whenever possible.*

recognized one aspect of the job they liked and were skillful at and made sure the employee engaged in that aspect of the job at least once a day.

Whatever the cause for poor attitudes, a supervisor may be able to influence that attitude, but will almost never have complete control over such problem attitudes.

Behaviors

Unlike attitudes, which can be subjective and based on feelings, behaviors are easier to detect and correct. Behaviors are an observable act. They are actions, errors, omissions, or words that are observed (seen or heard) by a supervisor. Behaviors can also come to the attention of a supervisor when a supervisor observes the results or consequences of an employee's actions, errors, omissions, or words.

Imagine one of your employees arriving to work 20 minutes late for a shift. The employee is wearing a dirty uniform that includes missing required items (i.e. a badge and name tag) and is wearing an

> *Behaviors are an observable act. They are actions, errors, omissions, or words observed (seen or heard) by a supervisor.*

unauthorized jacket and hat. Imagine that when you attempt to talk to the employee about being late and about his appearance, he raises his voice, starts swearing at you and walks away while yelling to his coworkers how much he hates his job. Your first thoughts may be that this is a disrespectful, unprofessional employee with a poor attitude. You may be right, especially if this is not the first time this has happened. The problem is that if your response targets his attitude, your correction will probably be unsuccessful. With behaviors, however, you manage the behavior to make sure it is not repeated.

Tardiness is a behavior. What employees wear as part of the required uniform, and how they wear it, is a behavior. Disrespectful or offensive language is a behavior. Supervisors may not be able to fix or even adjust attitudes as much as they like, but they can manage, correct, and even require improvement regarding behaviors.

A Different Mindset

Imagine an employee you observe sleeping on the job. The employee could have a poor attitude. But whether you ignore the problem in hopes the problem fixes itself, or whether your approach is to yell and "put the fear of God" into the employee, you are not likely to change the employee's poor attitude. So do not make your response about the attitude.

Now this sleeping employee could also be one of your best workers with an excellent attitude. Even good employees occasionally do stupid things. When you wake the employee and confront him about sleeping,

> *Even good employees occasionally do stupid things. Your mindset in addressing that behavior can mean the difference between earning employee commitment or creating a problem employee.*

the employee may explain the many reasons he is overly tired. He worked a double shift. His newborn kept him awake the night before, and he has only gotten a few hours sleep all week. The employee admits he is so tired he cannot keep his eyes open and that is why you found him sleeping behind the wheel of his parked police cruiser. In such a case, it might have been helpful if you had previously given the employee this clearly stated expectation.

"If you encounter issues on or off the job that impact either your wellbeing or your ability to perform to your usual high standards, please let me know."

Rather than threatening the employee with discipline or punishment or yelling at him in hopes of an attitude adjustment, you should focus on the behavior that you observed. You observed the employee sleeping—a capable employee unable to stay awake. You advise the employee it is clearly unsafe to sleep on the job—especially in a parked police cruiser. One of your jobs, as a supervisor, is to help keep employees safe. You cannot keep them safe if you do not have all the information you need about their well-being on any given day.

If you had given him an expectation in advance, you could focus on the expectation that clearly told him to let you know if anything was going on in his life that might affect his job and his safety. An employee who cannot stay awake on the job due to the fact he did not get enough sleep because his baby kept him awake for the past few nights, is one of those situations that might be helpful for a supervisor to know.

Better Results

The above situation was a real-life scenario in which a supervisor ultimately directed the employee to take a sick day for the rest of the shift. The supervisor told me he focused on the behavior that he observed rather than the employee's attitude. He said he clarified that he would not tolerate sleeping on his shift, because it was not safe. He emphasized that he wanted the employee to make him aware of any circumstances that might affect the employee's ability to perform his duties. The supervisor advised me that the results were twofold. First, it stopped people from sleeping on duty on the shift he supervised. Second, employees (especially the involved employee) came to understand that this supervisor cared about their safety and well-being much more than he cared about disciplining or punishing employees. Employees became more committed to the supervisor—meeting his expectations—not because they feared his disciplinary wrath, but because they did not want to let him down or disappoint this supervisor who they came to trust and respect.

CHAPTER 14

Delivering Feedback

Feedback can be informal or formal. It can be in the form of recognition, or in the form of criticism, correction, or a requirement to improve. Feedback can even be neutral (meaning neither recognition nor criticism) when it provides instruction, direction, or just an opportunity for job-related interaction between a subordinate and a supervisor. Supervisors attempting to provide feedback to their employees should consider the following guidelines.

Focus on behaviors, not attitudes. Employee attitudes can frustrate and aggravate supervisors but are difficult, if not impossible, to correct. Fortunately, within almost every attitude problem, there are observable behaviors. Focus your energies and efforts on correcting or improving behaviors. Please note that job performance is a behavior, not an attitude. While attitude categories may exist in some performance evaluations or in performance-tracking computer software, refrain from writing narratives that discuss or require attitude improvement. A performance evaluation entry that states "You need to improve your attitude" is subjective and difficult, if not impossible, to measure. Reword your narrative to describe observed or expected behaviors.

Be specific. Telling an employee that they are always late for work or never get their reports in on time is seldom helpful or accurate. Be specific about the behavior that you observe that deserves recognition or criticism or requires improvement. Generic statements like "sometime" or "most of the time" do not help correct behavior.

Offer solutions when needed, not just criticism.
Employees make mistakes or fail to do what you ask because of one of three things: they lack resources; they lack knowledge; or they lack desire. A lack of resources (manpower or equipment) might be a legitimate reason for the employee's failure, and a supervisor might help in addressing that problem. A lack of knowledge may be corrected by formal training or on-the-job instruction. But some employees lack the desire to do the job, and additional resources or more training will not likely fix a lack of desire. Criticism and correction may be warranted, but often what is needed most is a caring supervisor that helps find a solution to the problem, or at least helps the employee find a solution.

Face-to-face. Email is a useful communication tool. But like any tool, it should be used only in the right situation. Email serves as a valuable way to share general information. It can also be used as a supplemental method of reaching out to employees to recognize their exemplary work. Email, however, should not be used to provide so-called constructive criticism, negative feedback, or complaints about behavior and performance. Too often, supervisors develop "email courage" and say things they would never say face-to-face to an employee.

When a supervisor feels it is necessary to provide negative feedback to suggest or require improvement, or when it is necessary to point out mistakes to prevent them from reoccurring, then face-to-face communication should be used. Supervisors should avoid engaging in back-and-forth emails with their subordinates trying to clarify their intended meaning. All too often, subordinates receive emails that convey a sense of anger without clear direction. Well-intended emails can be misunderstood, resulting in a loss of trust.

When you need to provide negative feedback or you need to reiterate expectations to one employee, face-to-face, in-person feedback provides the clearest form of communication. Face-to-face feedback allows your subordinates to hear not only the words spoken, but the tone in which they are delivered. Nuances in tone and body language (so essential to the real meaning of your message) are lost when you communicate by email.

Besides increasing the effectiveness of your feedback delivery, face-to-face feedback allows you the opportunity to observe your subordinate's response. Those observations are not possible by email. In fact, supervisors often report that subordinates do not always respond to negative emails. Whether this failure to respond is due to an effort to avoid conflict, a sign of disrespect, or whether the subordinate views the received email as a joke depends on the supervisor and the situation. Clearly, emails are less effective than face-to-face communication.

No Email Tag. One last thought on email communications. A subordinate may try to bait or manipulate a supervisor by sending emails with aggravating comments or questions. Do not get sucked into playing email tag with subordinates. The best response to such emails is, "Come and see me when you get a chance." Let the employee know you are willing to have a discussion, just not by email. The same holds true if you need to email a subordinate about a problem. Send them an email saying, "Please come and see me when you have a chance." You can provide a few details to keep them from guessing, but do not get into a lengthy explanation that just encourages another round of email tag. Your purpose for the email is to contact the employee to come and see you, so you can have the discussion face-to-face.

Empathy—be aware of your impact. Whether supervisors call it constructive criticism or negative feedback, such discussions feel like criticism to your employees. They may or may not acknowledge that criticism or correction is warranted. Some employees will deny they made a mistake, even in the face of clear and convincing consequences that resulted from that mistake. Some will play the blame game, some will be embarrassed, and a few might worry about job security. Some employees will handle criticism better than others. They may take it personally and even become confrontational. Understand that for most people it is difficult to admit mistakes and most dislike being told that they need improvement.

Keep your goal in mind. It is important to understand that your feedback may not always be appreciated by that employee. It is essential to maintain your professionalism throughout the discussion. These discussions are not an opportunity to show that you are in charge or to get your "pound of flesh" by yelling or embarrassing the employee.

Your goal in providing any negative or corrective feedback is simply to improve their future behavior. Ideally, you identify the problem and help the employee correct the problem, so you do not have to repeat the same discussion in the future. While it might be nice if the employee apologized, apologies are not always appropriate. And even when apologies are given, they do not always fix the situation. Do not expect apologies from subordinates in most situations. Even so, it is fair to expect that the employee understands your meaning and expectations. When the meeting is over, the employee does not necessarily have to leave happy, but they should be able to leave with their self-respect in place.

Short and sweet (or at least concise and professional). A few words of caution regarding how supervisors should conduct meetings where they are trying to improve employee behavior or performance. Be courteous and professional from the start, but skip the fluff—those pointless, feel-good conversations that you think will make the "criticism pill" easier to swallow. Likewise, end the meeting with courtesy and professionalism while avoiding watering down your message. Closing comments such as, "I hope you know I am just doing my job" or "It's not that big of a deal" water down your message and make the point of your feedback seem meaningless.

Occasionally, an employee did a great job at something unrelated to your corrective feedback. You might think it a perfect opportunity to give recognition at the same meeting to balance out the negative feedback just delivered. Do not confuse your message. You are not discussing the employee's overall behavior or performance. You are discussing a specific situation that you want to prevent from repeating. Save your recognition for a separate meeting. It is likely that the employee may be upset regarding your negative comments and will miss your well-intentioned recognition. Those moments when you can give recognition happen so seldom that you do not want to waste the opportunity by trying to give it at the same time you are giving corrective feedback. Keep those two discussions separate.

CHAPTER 15

Documentation

The word "documentation" often implies a negative connotation. When employees hear that something about their behavior or performance is being documented, they assume that something negative is being entered in their personnel file. As mentioned earlier in this book, supervisors often delay having crucial conversations with their employees for a variety of reasons, including a natural tendency towards conflict avoidance. Documentation regarding performance and behavior is often delayed— even longer than those difficult discussions.

There is an old adage that goes something like this: *If it isn't documented, it didn't happen.* For traditional progressive discipline, that adage is true. I have lost count on the number of supervisors who have told me stories about problem employees whose egregious behaviors aggravated and frustrated them for years. Often, one final incident tips the scale and the administration becomes fed up enough to impose formal discipline or even termination. It is then that they realize that while internal historical knowledge of the employee's problem is well known, formal documentation is minimal or nonexistent. The administration is then forced to start from scratch documenting the employee's long-standing problem behavior. If anecdotal evidence is worth anything, it is clear that most supervisors, organization-wide and at every level, could do better job at documentation.

Performance Tracking Software

To improve documenting both excellent and poor performance or behavior, many organizations have acquired performance-tracking computer software. This software allows supervisors at every level to input observations about their subordinates' behavior and performance. But the data ultimately received from any performance-tracking software is only as reliable as the data that is entered.

Despite training and careful planning (and in some cases mandated policies) on what is required to be entered and when, opinions still vary among individual supervisors about what should be entered. In some cases, supervisors enter only positive comments. Some supervisors even go out of their way to enter a lot of positive, if not exaggerated, comments. Other supervisors only enter negative comments. Supervisors who believe that subordinates should mirror their enthusiasm and productivity might enter more criticism than other supervisors. And, of course, there are supervisors who think the entire concept of performance tracking is a conspiracy by the administration, and so they enter as little as possible.

If used as intended, performance-tracking computer software has great potential and can be an especially useful documentation tool. But like performance evaluations, or any written documentation that will become a part of an employee's record, what is entered needs to be monitored by those who supervise the supervisor. There should be a supervisory overview of a supervisor's documentation proficiency to minimize the occurrence of inappropriate documentation trends.

> *The results obtained from performance tracking software are only as good as the data that is entered by supervisors.*

Emphasizing or exaggerating an employee's positive traits, while ignoring obvious problems, does a disservice to the employee and the organization. Likewise, unjustifiably harsh, critical, or vindictive documentation entries are unfair. The information recorded in performance-tracking software is only useful if it is an accurate reflection of a supervisor's observations.

For those organizations using performance-tracking computer software, anecdotal evidence suggests even when certain entries are mandated, wide discretion still exists. Supervisors may hesitate to make an entry for the first, second, or even third occurrence of an inappropriate behavior. Because of this tendency, it makes sense for supervisors to consider using documentation or "supervisor's notes" not as an alternative to an organization's formal documentation practices, but as a supplement to that process.

Supervisor's Notes

It is important at this point to emphasize that informal documentation or supervisor's notes should never circumvent an organization's formal or required documentation procedures. Neither should it be used to avoid an organization's formal progressive discipline when such actions are appropriate. Supervisor's notes serve one purpose and that is to give the supervisor an added tool to help get the best possible behavior and performance from an individual employee.

> *Supervisor's notes are a tool to help supervisors get the best possible behavior and performance from their employees.*

Supervisor's notes record key events in employee behavior and performance—both good and bad. The intent is to use those notes as a productive tool so that before a supervisor meets with an employee, the supervisor can review the notes to refresh his or her memory and have a more productive meeting with the employee.

Supervisor's notes also document what you have done to help the employee correct a problem or improve their behavior or performance. If you have a problem employee with issues that you cannot resolve yourself, and you go to your supervisor for help, it is likely that your supervisor will ask you what you have done to correct the problem. It may be beneficial to have notes regarding the dates and purpose of various meetings you had with the employee as you tried to help the employee meet your expectations.

For organizations conducting annual performance evaluations, supervisor's notes may support accurate performance ratings. Some organizations require supporting notations for performance evaluations to be more formalized on department mandated forms. But in absence of more formal requirements, supervisors who try to recall a year's worth of employee behavior and performance from memory might be better served by using supervisor's notes to help refresh their memory.

Not Discipline

Supervisor's notes are not (or should not be) considered discipline and should not be part of the employee's personnel file. Here is where the argument usually begins regarding supervisor's notes. Some will argue that a supervisor cannot keep notes outside the personnel file, that they are secret notes used to harm the employee and, therefore, are prohibited.

If what you are writing is discipline, then the employee must see what you have written. And such documentation becomes a part of the employee's personnel file. That disciplinary documentation is used as part of the organization's progressive discipline process, meaning that subsequent documentation for a similar occurrence could result in more severe consequences. Such disciplinary documentation differs significantly from supervisor's notes.

If you have several meetings with an employee about performance and you make notes for yourself about what occurred at those meetings, and those notes are used only to refresh your memory should future meetings be needed, that is not discipline. Only formal documentation in the employee's personnel file can be used as part of progressive discipline.

What to Include and What Not to Include

Include facts regarding behavior and performance that you feel are noteworthy (both good and bad) that might be beneficial for you to recall at a future date to help the employee improve or reach their maximum potential. Avoid conjecture and opinion in your notations. Write nothing in your supervisor's notes that you have not already discussed with the employee. Write nothing in your notes that would embarrass you, if it were read by the employee, by your supervisor, or by anyone else. And, if you have any doubt about whether supervisor's notes can be used in your organization, check with your administration, human resource director, or legal counsel.

> *Write nothing in your notes that you have not already discussed with your employee.*

What if an employee wants to see what you have written? If asked, the employee can see the notes you have taken regarding your actions with that specific employee. What if the notes get subpoenaed? It does not matter if an employee, the union, or a court wants to see your supervisor's notes. You will never write anything in those notes that is not factual and that you have not already discussed with the employee. You will never write anything in those notes that will embarrass you if those notes were read by others. Those notes will only reflect what you have observed and what you have done to help the employee.

No Signature Required

Some supervisors have suggested that the only notes a supervisor should take are those that are shown to the employee and acknowledged by the employee with the signature. I have encountered organizations where such a practice exists. In talking to supervisors in those organizations, they tell me few, if any, such notes are taken. It is like giving somebody a verbal warning, but then telling them to sign a document while you try to convince them "Don't worry, it's just a verbal warning that I am making you sign and putting in your personnel file." It would be difficult convincing an employee not to worry about that documentation. Supervisors know the anxiety it causes and avoid such documentation like the plague. When supervisors in such organizations are asked why they did not document a behavior, the most frequent answer is that the circumstance did not rise to a level that justified documentation requiring an employee's signature. They would rather avoid the conflict than benefit from a supervisor's note that requires a signature.

The supervisor's notes that I am suggesting are designed to help the supervisor do his or her job while producing the least amount of anxiety for both the supervisor and the employee. Listed on the following pages are three options for supervisor's notes or informal documentation that might be utilized outside of an organization's performance-tracking software and outside of an employee's personnel file. These include a basic supervisor's note, a performance log, and a discussion summary sent by email.

Three Types of Informal Documentation

The Basic Supervisor's Note

A simple supervisor's note is probably the easiest type of informal supervisor documentation to maintain. It can be done in a computer program, or "old-school" in a notebook. It contains the date and time, the satisfactory or unacceptable behavior or performance observed, the supervisor's actions, and the employee's response or commitment to change.

An Example of a Supervisor's Note

> 09/02/20 Supervisor's Note
> 4:30pm
>
> Met with Officer Smith regarding being 20 minutes late for his shift today. He explained he over-slept and didn't think to call the station. I told him he must call and let me know if he was going to be late. He said in the future, he would call.

The Performance Log

A performance log can easily be maintained on a spreadsheet. The log includes a column for the date; a column for the situation (and whether the situation was positive, negative, or neutral); and a column for the outcome which are the results or action taken by the supervisor. The performance log provides a quick overview of the employee's noteworthy behavior and performance whether it be excellent, unsatisfactory, or somewhere in-between.

An Example of a Performance Log

Date	Situation *Positive, Negative, Neutral*	Outcome *Results/Action Taken*
09/02/20	John was 20 minutes late for his shift today and did not call to let me know.	I discussed the issue with John. He said he over-slept and didn't think to call the station. I told him he must call and let me know if he was going to be late. He said in the future, he would call.
09/05/20	Received a call from Mrs. Jones that John had gone out of his way to help her at the call to her business yesterday and that he was courteous and professional.	I told John about the call and thanked him for his great work on the call. I also emailed the chief about the call.

Discussion Summary by Email

Email automatically records the date and time. The contents of the email are a summary of the meeting between the supervisor and the employee. It can include the supervisor's observations, actions taken, and commitment for change. It has the added advantage of allowing the employee to confirm the accuracy of any statements in the email by stating, "Please let me know if I omitted anything or there are any discrepancies in this discussion summary."

Discussion summaries by email are an excellent method of documenting performance discussions and reminding both the supervisor and the employee of what was said. Unlike the other two examples, this form of a supervisor's note advises the employee of your documentation efforts. This concept works great for some supervisors, but depending on the supervisor and the employee, it may not be the perfect strategy for everyone.

An Example of a Discussion Summery Email

from: sgt@anytownpd.com
to: jsmith@anytownpd.com
date: Sept 02, 2020, 10:35am

I met with you today regarding being 20 minutes late for your shift today. You explained you over-slept and didn't think to call the station. I told you that I expect you to call and let me know if you are going to be late. You said in the future, you would call. Please let me know if I omitted anything or there are any errors in this discussion summary.

Formal Documentation

For progressive discipline, the documentation that is most appropriate and often required is formal documentation. Formal documentation includes, but is not limited to, letters of reprimand that become part of the employee's personnel file. Informal supervisor's notes, and even performance-tracking software entries should give supervisors tools to help their employees improve behavior and performance. Still, some issues are serious enough to warrant formal documentation in the employee's personnel file even for the first occurrence. Formal documentation is also used for repeated inappropriate behavior or substandard performance (even of a minor nature) when a supervisor's repeated efforts have failed to achieve correction or improvement.

Supervisors are hesitant to start formal documentation unless a serious incident has occurred, or they have become frustrated with the employee's refusal to heed their advice or direction. Supervisors should not rush to judgment when it comes to documentation that will be placed in an employee's personnel file. Such documentation, even for minor occurrences, can have serious implications on the employee's future within the organization. But supervisors must also have the courage to formally document serious occurrences, or minor occurrences of a repeated nature, when appropriate.

It is important that supervisors care about the well-being of their employees. To that end, it is hoped that they work with the employee prior to the formal documentation to try to correct minor, but repeated, occurrences. But when all other efforts fail, at times formal documentation and progressive discipline are the correct choice. In addition, occasionally, even typically good employees make poor decisions that are serious enough to warrant formal documentation even for a first occurrence.

The Goal is to Change Behavior

Even though an employee may view formal documentation as discipline (and that may be an accurate belief), the goal in almost every case is the same as informal documentation. Supervisors document employee performance and behavior in hopes of improving both. Unless the employee is being terminated, supervisors should not give up on the employee simply because formal documentation is initiated. The employee should be encouraged not to view such documentation as the end of their career, but as an opportunity to make corrections.

Not every mistake, inappropriate behavior, or substandard performance needs to be recorded formally and placed in the employee's personnel file. But do not kid yourself thinking informal measures will always fix employee problems. Occasionally, formal progressive discipline is the correct response to a problem. Documentation in the form of written warnings, documented counseling, letters of reprimand, or other components of an organization's progressive discipline system are sometimes the only logical option.

CHAPTER 16

Coaching

Every employee wants to know two things from their supervisor. First, they want to know what is expected of them on the job. Second, they want to know how the supervisor thinks they are doing at meeting those expectations. It is the ethical obligation of every supervisor to provide answers to those two questions. Those answers can come in the form of either informal or formal feedback.

In organizations using annual performance evaluations, too often the answers to those two important questions are discovered by the employee only upon receiving their evaluation. Whether your agency uses performance evaluations or not, coaching minimizes those surprises by providing supervisors with an opportunity to give essential feedback to their employees to help improve their performance.

Calendar-Driven Coaching
In calendar-driven coaching, the supervisor schedules the employee coaching session in advance—even if there are no significant issues or problems. Some agencies hold

regularly scheduled coaching sessions halfway through their performance evaluation period. A growing practice among law enforcement agencies is for immediate supervisors to schedule regular monthly coaching sessions with individual subordinates. To some, this sounds like a burdensome task. But please note, a coaching session can be relatively brief, and simply serves as a format to provide feedback that should already be occurring regularly.

During these regularly scheduled coaching sessions, supervisors should discuss their expectations, and how they think the employee is doing at meeting those expectations. The supervisor can also review any recent significant events, cases, employee accomplishments, or performance issues observed by the supervisor. The supervisor might end the coaching session by asking the employee if there is anything he or she can do to make the employee's job easier. Why would a supervisor ask such a question? It is simply another way of encouraging feedback from a subordinate to help you decide if you should modify your leadership efforts so you can get the best possible performance from your employees.

Event-Driven Coaching

Event-driven coaching sessions typically are held after any event that the supervisor believes warrants discussion, review, correction, improvement, or recognition. This could include the completion of a major assignment or case, an employee encountering a problem on the job, or an employee expressing frustration or dissatisfaction with the job. The problem could be the tasks assigned, the workload, a lack of training, skills, or ability, or even a problem with a coworker. All these issues can affect job performance and morale of the employee and the employee's coworkers.

Finally, event-driven coaching sessions are appropriate any time an employee's attitude worsens significantly from the norm for that individual employee and that negative change lasts for more than a few days. While supervisors are advised to focus on behaviors rather than attitudes, a sudden negative change in attitude may be a symptom of a larger underlying problem that deserves your attention.

Coaching Basics

Supervisors should utilize both calendar-driven and event-driven coaching sessions. This combination gives supervisors multiple opportunities to help improve employee performance. In addition to providing advice and support, coaching sessions can be used by a supervisor to build two things that are closely related: employee confidence and employee competence.

Coaching sessions are extremely useful in the overall improvement of employee performance and in the development of a strong working relationship between the supervisor and the employee. But it should be understood that coaching is not counseling.

Some agencies use the terms coaching and counseling interchangeably. However, many agencies use formal counseling as part of their disciplinary process. Coaching is not intended to be discipline. In fact, coaching sessions help prevent the need for discipline.

Coaching is also not intended to replace needed personal counseling for mental health, drug and alcohol, PTSD, or other personal issues. Those issues require professional counseling that is far beyond the scope of coaching. If an employee is in need of such counseling, provide the employee with the appropriate resources, which may include the agency's employee assistance program or referral to appropriate outside professional counseling.

CHAPTER 17

Performance Discussions

Most feedback comes in the form of casual conversations or coaching. A small percentage of feedback occurs during formal disciplinary action. In-between those two extremes there is the *performance discussion*. A performance discussion is a semiformal discussion between a supervisor and an employee that can be used to help correct a problem before formal discipline is needed. Performance discussions often occur during either calendar-driven or event-driven coaching sessions discussed in the previous chapter.

When to use Performance Discussions
Performance discussions occur after more casual or informal conversations fail to correct an observed employee problem—often, but not always—during a coaching session. Performance discussions are similar—if not identical—to what some organizations refer to as formal counseling. Many organizations consider *counseling* formal discipline, requiring documentation in the employee's personnel file. Performance discussions give

supervisors a semiformal alternative with no requirement to make an entry in the employee's personal file.

If your organization requires all such discussions to be recorded in the employee's personnel file, please follow your organization's requirements. Unfortunately, wherever such mandates exist, they usually result in less utilization of this useful process. This is especially true for supervisors hoping to avoid conflicts that arise when formal documentation is seen as punishment by the employee.

A better way to document performance discussions might be to use supervisor's notes, as previously discussed. Those notes document the actions taken by the supervisor and the commitment to change given by the employee. Documentation serves as a reminder to the supervisor should subsequent discussions become necessary. If the behavior or performance does not improve, consider formal documentation in the subordinate's personnel file as part of the progressive discipline process. Starting the formal disciplinary process is always an option but is not always an appropriate first course of action.

How many Performance Discussions?

A single performance discussion might do the trick. But you may need a follow-up discussion to change a long-tolerated or long-ignored unacceptable behavior. It is up to you to decide if failure to comply should require another performance discussion or more formal actions, including initiation of formal progressive discipline. While you may need to hold multiple performance discussions, at some point you should conclude that noncompliance is not because of a misunderstanding, but a refusal to change. In such cases, the performance discussions should stop, and more formal procedures should be initiated.

Why Performance Discussions Work

Performance discussions work because they alleviate all misunderstanding regarding the problem or issue being discussed. They also remove any question as to your expectations. Be specific about the performance or behavior you observed that must change. The performance discussion ends with you asking for the subordinate's commitment to change or improve. The subordinate gives his or her word (nothing need be in writing) that the change will occur and that the problem will not be repeated. There is little wiggle room after a performance discussion for a subordinate to claim he or she did not know what you meant or wanted. And there are few plausible excuses for failure to comply. Failure to comply means that the subordinate broke his or her word to you.

Subsequent Performance Discussions

If subsequent performance discussions are needed, they should focus on the fact that the subordinate gave—and did not keep his or her word. The initial unacceptable behavior or poor performance becomes secondary to the issue of trust. Going forward, can you trust the employee's word and their stated commitment to make the necessary changes? If you can, maybe another performance discussion is worth the effort. If not, consider more formal alternatives.

The Seven-Step Process

The performance discussion is an easy-to-use practical feedback process that will give you better results than repeated casual conversations. It is an ideal tool for when the problem behavior does not yet merit more formal disciplinary measures. Listed below are the seven steps of the performance discussion process.

1. **Identify the Specific Problem Behavior.**
   - Pick the most significant issue to address. It is likely that—by the time you are frustrated enough with a problem employee to have a performance discussion—you have a lengthy list of issues you want to discuss with that employee. Pick the most significant issue at that moment to discuss. If you add numerous issues to your list, it will feel to the employee like you are piling on complaints. Your subsequent discussion will feel more like a lecture than a performance discussion. And today's employees have become skilled at tuning out lectures. Remember, this discussion is about correcting a problem, not venting about a list of issues that have frustrated you for years.

   - Take the time to write out what you believe the problem is in a concise written explanation—just a few sentences. Use this to help you prepare for the discussion. If your written explanation is concise and you identified the specific issue, the problem will be easy for the employee to understand and correct. If your written explanation looks like a college essay, consider rethinking the problem to make it more concise and to the point.

- Review what you have written. Does it describe an attitude or a behavior? Focus on behaviors. If your explanation describes an attitude, reword it so it describes an observable behavior. This is not to suggest that the attitude problem is not legitimate, but attitudes are subjective and hard to measure, even if corrected. Reword your problem statement so that what you are describing is an observed behavior.

- Determine if what you have written describes a problem that is specific enough to change. Avoid nonspecific phrases. Avoid discussing motivation, being a *team-player*, being more *friendly*, or other words or terms that are subjective. Stick to observable behaviors that are specific enough for the employee to clearly understand.

- Make sure you have the authority to require the behavioral change you are requesting. A supervisor might have a pet peeve or strong belief which they follow, but for which they have no authority to hold others accountable. Your accountability efforts might even be thwarted by your supervisor who does not agree with a policy or your expectations. If you suspect this may occur, consider talking to your supervisor first to gain their support—or at least find out where they stand—in case your subordinate goes over your head.

2. **Determine the Performance Gap.**
Compare your expectations against the employee's actual performance. What is your expectation or desired result? What is the actual observed behavior? What needs to be done to close the gap?

3. **Determine the Impact.**
What is the impact of the employee's behavior or performance on coworkers, you, the organization, or the mission? If the employee's actions or behaviors impact the morale of other employees, then it affects performance. Chronic negativity spreads like a disease. Rule breakers, rule benders, lazy or incompetent employees, and those contributing to a toxic work environment all impact the motivation, morale, and performance of other employees. You do not always have to explain the impact to the employee. But you should be aware of the impact in case you decide to bring it up during the discussion.

4. Determine Consequences.

What are the potential consequences if the employee
refuses to change? You do not always need to explain
the potential consequences, but you need to know what
they are in case the employee asks. There are at least
four potential consequences.

- Failure to change or improve may cause the loss of
  respect by the employee's coworkers.

- Failure to change or improve could result in
  additional supervision. Some employees need more
  management than leadership.

- Failure to change or improve may be reflected in
  the employee's annual performance evaluation.

- Failure to change or improve could result in formal
  progressive discipline.

5. Create a Plan.

Most behavior and performance problems are not
emergencies. In fact, you have probably been aware of
issues with one or more of your problem employees for
a long time. Most of these situations will allow you a
little time to create a plan that will increase the
likelihood of success. Review what you have written
so you understand what you plan to say. But do not
read it to the employee. Your written explanation is

only to help you prepare. Plan for not only what you will say, but the employee's likely response.

If your performance discussion will be with a confrontational employee, play "devil's advocate" and consider the employees likely excuses, confrontational responses, and blame shifting he or she is likely to attempt. Consider all your emotional "hot buttons." If you know them in advance, they will have less power over you if mentioned by the employee. What are the things a confrontational employee could say to you that might affect your emotions? The more emotional you become during a performance discussion, the more your logic and professionalism will decline. Planning can alleviate some of these problems.

6. **Have the Performance Discussion.**
   If you have done a little advanced planning, the actual performance discussion could be the easiest part of this entire process. Have the discussion in a private formal or semiformal setting. Give specific feedback on the problem you identified. Stick with one issue per discussion. This is about changing behavior, not reading a laundry list of past problems. You can allow an opportunity for the employee to give an explanation, but excuses should be kept to a minimum. You can discuss the impact caused by the employee's current behavior, and the consequences that could result from a refusal to change if you so desire.

The performance discussion ends with you asking for and receiving a commitment from the employee to change. "Can you take care of that for me, so we don't have this problem again?" A simple *yes* answer or similar verbal commitment to change is the response required. There is no need for repeated assurances or signed documents. All you are looking for is the employee's commitment to meet your expectations.

When the performance discussion is over, do not harp on other issues, issue threats, or water-down this important discussion. It is not the time to give recognition for a positive occurrence that happened the day before. Nor is it the time to have a friendly conversation about what the employee is doing for fun this coming weekend. Trust-building casual conversations and engagement opportunities are important. So, too, is recognizing employees who do excellent work. Nevertheless, there is an appropriate time and place for every type of conversation. Performance discussions are about changing behavior and performance. Save those valuable trust-building moments for a different time and place.

7. Follow-up.

The follow-up is one of the most important aspects of a performance discussion, and it is a step that is often overlooked. If the behavior changes, acknowledge it by giving recognition for the positive change. Too few supervisors follow this advice. Supervisors are often quick to criticize when the behavior does not change, but often ignore satisfactory behavior because it is expected. If the employee did what you asked, acknowledge the positive change. Especially when the employee did exactly what they said they would do. Your follow-up lets the employee know that you care enough to pay attention to their success.

If the behavior or performance does not change, another performance discussion is an option. Although subsequent performance discussions should focus primarily on the fact that the employee did not keep his or her word. The initial issue is still important, but trust now becomes the primary issue. Can you trust the employee? Does the employee care if you trust them? At some point, if you cannot trust the employee or the employee does not care about your trust, or claims not to care about consequences, you have few alternatives. Your final option is to proceed with formal discipline.

If you have not previously explained the potential consequences for failure or refusal to change to the employee, now is the time to explain the most significant potential consequence. Advise the employee that this is the one consequence that you had hoped to avoid by having the performance discussion. It is up to you if you want to give the employee one last chance to honor their commitment to change or improve. Nevertheless, at some point, unproductive performance discussions should stop, and progressive discipline should begin.

EXAMPLE: How you might use the 7 *Step Process* to address a gossip problem.

1. **Identify the Specific Problem Behavior.**
   I observed an employee engaging in gossip—making derogatory comments and engaging in character-assassination of a coworker who was not present to defend himself.

2. **Determine the Performance Gap.**
   I expect my subordinates to treat each other with dignity and respect and communicated that expectation in writing to all employees. On three occasions, I observed the employee making disparaging comments about a coworker who was not present to defend himself (the employee clearly engaged in gossip).

3. **Determine Impact.**
   The incident resulted in morale problems, coworker conflict on the shift, and a loss of productivity.

4. **Determine Consequences.**
   The possible consequences for this employee include a loss of respect by coworkers, additional supervision to require minimum behavior and performance standards, poor performance evaluation ratings, and progressive discipline.

5. **Create a Plan.**

   I plan to hold a performance discussion with the employee using assertive communication. I will tell the employee, "I overheard what you said. It was inappropriate, and I will not tolerate gossip on the shift." The planned discussion will be brief and to the point. I will ensure that the behavior I discuss and the future behavior I request is specific.

6. **Have a Performance Discussion.**

   I will meet privately with the employee to discuss my expectations, the employee's current performance, and if necessary, an explanation of possible consequences for failure to meet my expectations.

7. **Follow-up.**

   At regular intervals, I will advise the employee he is meeting, or failing to meet, the expectations discussed in the performance discussion. If there is no repeat of the problem behavior this week, I will thank the employee for taking care of the problem we discussed (even if I am not positive the problem is permanently resolved). I will give feedback on what I observe. If I observe the employee engage in gossip again, I will hold another performance discussion without delay.

CHAPTER 18

Clear Communications

The clarity and effectiveness with which you communicate can affect what others believe about you and your character. Fortunately, communication clarity is a learned skill. That means that whatever natural communication abilities you were born with, you can get even better with practice.

Do not underestimate the importance of clear communication. Done correctly, clear communication allows you to convey necessary instructions and expectations to subordinates, while avoiding hidden meanings. Clear communication helps you hold employees accountable without appearing mean-spirited or vindictive. Clear communication helps you convey appreciation in the form of recognition to your employees for doing a good job. Clear communication helps you build trust, but it is more than your ability to build trust that is at stake. Clear communication helps you influence your employees, and it is your influence that helps employees reach their maximum potential.

The acronym **C.L.E.A.R.** may help you remember the essential elements of clear communications.

C - Conversations

Casual conversations are an important strategy in the trust-building process. Unfortunately, too many people believe that a conversation is taking place when one person is talking and another is listening. That is probably more accurately described as storytelling. And it is a natural tendency, when one person is telling a story, that the other person, rather than listening, is planning a response.

Do yourself a favor—avoid trying to one-up that person by coming up with a better story. Dale Carnegie wrote long ago in his book, *How to Win Friends and Influence People,* that if you want to become an interesting person, you need to show an interest in others. The best way to show an interest in your employees is to ask them questions—ask them questions about things important to them. Those questions could be about work, their family, their hobbies, or what they did for fun last weekend.

While questions are an appropriate way to show your interest, follow-up questions can make you a conversational expert. A simple "How was your vacation?" is a nice way to show you care about an employee returning from a week-long vacation. However, following that question with follow-up questions such as, "Did you like it there? What was it like? Did you have fun?" shows you are not just giving a robotic obligatory response to an employee. You

are showing you are interested and care about that
employee.

L - Listen

When listening to a subordinate's ideas, questions, career
aspirations, concerns, complaints, or even what they did
last weekend, it is important to take the time to pay
attention. But really listening requires more than just going
through the motions or looking at a person and occasionally
nodding your head while they talk. Real listening requires
effort. It requires you to hear what and how something is
said, while observing the body language to help you better
understand the message.

Real listening requires focused attention. That means
stop what you are doing and face the person who is talking
to you. Avoid trying to talk over your shoulder while
walking away. Avoid looking at your watch, the clock on
the wall, or the activity going on behind the person.
Maintain eye contact and respond appropriately, verbally,
and with the appropriate body language.

Focused attention means stop multitasking! It may
be physically possible to answer your phone, send a text
message, or continue typing on your computer while
talking. But multitasking comes across as disrespectful to
the person trying to talk to you. Your multitasking sends
them a signal that they do not deserve 100% of your
attention.

Instead of multitasking, consider one of two options.
You can stop the task, face your subordinate, and give them

your focused and undivided attention during the discussion. The alternative is that if you are engaged in a critical task and pressed for time, you can ask the employee if you could meet at a later specified time to have the discussion. One note of caution, supervisors often mistakenly believe that most of the tasks they are working on require their immediate and focused attention. If in fact, your task must be done now, focus on the task. But if the task can be delayed briefly, have the conversation with your employee. If you do decide to delay the conversation, make sure the employee is not experiencing an emergency that requires your immediate attention. Focus on your employee or focus on your task. Do not try to do both at the same time.

Finally, if an employee comes to you with a legitimate concern or complaint, do more than just listen. Listening is a great start, but some problems require action. Even if it is a situation that you cannot resolve yourself, take action to make sure the appropriate person addresses or is at least aware of the problem. An open-door policy, or claiming you are always willing to listen to your employees, quickly becomes a meaningless gesture if you repeatedly fail to address the concerns they bring to your attention.

E - Engage
Engaging and interacting with employees is one of the most effective trust-building strategies that a supervisor can undertake. Best of all, it is entirely free. The only cost is a little effort and knowing how and when to engage.

Supervisors can start improving their engagement efforts
by being open to informal conversation. For some
supervisors, this concept will be easier than for others. If
you are a task-focused
supervisor, you may
initially question the
value of casual
conversations unrelated
to work. You might view
such conversations as an

> One of the most critical skills
> of leadership is developing the
> mind-set that consistently
> engaging others is important.
> —Jack Enter, Ph.D.

attempt by employees to shirk their duties, and you might
feel a little guilty yourself by either engaging in or allowing
such conversations to occur.

It is important to know that some of the most effective
trust-building moments you will ever achieve with your
employees will occur during casual informal conversations.
It is during such conversations that employees talk about
the things in life that are most important to them. A
supervisor who understands that fact has the foundation for
building real employee trust and commitment.

What if a casual conversation goes on too long?
That happens occasionally. Being open to informal
conversations does not mean that such conversations
should replace the employee's duties. Inappropriately long
casual conversations, or even heated political debates
between coworkers, can interfere with work. On occasion,
supervisors have even been manipulated by employees who
realized a supervisor enjoyed talking about a topic. Such an
employee might engage in an inappropriately long

conversation to avoid or delay work. Like all trust-building efforts, skilled supervisors balance their efforts with the tasks and duties that employees are expected to complete.

Be open to the job-related input, opinions, and new ideas offered by your subordinates—regardless of their experience or time on the job. Some of the best ideas come from the least experienced employees, because they bring a new set of eyes to a problem. Being open to input, opinions, and ideas does not mean all their input is sound, or that you agree with all their opinions. But it is important that you listen to your employees. For every opinion you disagree with, and for every crazy new idea, there is a potential brilliant idea somewhere in your workforce just waiting to be shared.

You do not have to tell your employees that all their ideas are great. But after carefully listening, looking at the potential outcomes, and declining their idea, you need to respond. Your response should leave the employee with the feeling that even though you cannot adopt their idea at this time, they should feel encouraged to bring you their next new idea. Why? Because you are their supervisor and you want them to know that you expect ideas and input from those you supervise. And because it is your job to listen.

Look for opportunities to engage. Do not wait for employees to come to you. Your friends may come to you, chronic complainers may come to you, and those trying to brown-nose, or curry favor may come to you. That leaves a lot of other employees who will feel left out if you do not find ways to engage with them. And if you leave engagement to chance, waiting for the perfect opportunity or infrequent accidental contact, you will do yourself and your employees a disservice. It does not matter if your subordinates think the engagement was an accidental encounter or whether you created the opportunity. It just matters that the engagement occurs.

Accidental encounters do not have to be accidental. While not required, it is acceptable if encounters appear accidental or spontaneous to those with whom you wish to engage. If the encounter is accidental, see it as an opportunity and make sure you have something to say. Get to know your employees well enough that you can have a brief conversation with them (more than just saying hello) should such an opportunity arise. Employees have been known to marvel at the memorization ability of a supervisor who can converse about the employee's family and ask about the employee's children by name. It has more to do with planning than memory. Experienced supervisors take the time to do a little homework and refresh their memories as needed in preparation of both planned and accidental employee encounters.

Just being seen, giving a thumbs-up sign, or just saying "hello" is more than some supervisors attempt, and it may be better than nothing—but not by much. Real engagement means talking to employees about work-related and off-the-job related topics. It means talking to employees about things important to the employees as a way of showing you care about their well-being.

A - Assertive

An assertive communication style is the most preferred
communication style in almost every leadership situation.
But before I discuss assertive communication, let me
briefly discuss three other communication styles that cause
supervisors countless problems.

Passive Communications. Passive communicators hope
and wish for things to happen. They use the words "I hope"
or "I wish" when trying to suggest an employee behavior
they desire. "I *hope* everyone will be on time from now on.
I *wish* someone would answer that phone." Passive
communicators typically ignore issues that have a potential
for conflict. They give indirect or ambiguous responses and
blame their supervisor for directives or corrections they
give to subordinates.

If an employee is late for work, a passive
communicator might look at his or her watch hoping the
employee understands that they are upset instead of
discussing the tardiness. They might even use a little humor
about the possibility of the employee's watch being broken,
hoping the employee will understand the subtle message in
the humor and be on time the following day.

If one employee is late for work, it would not be
unusual for the passive communicator to email all
subordinates instructing everyone to be on time. Shotgun
comments or emails to a large group of employees may feel
less confrontational to the passive communicator than
interacting with an individual problem employee. But such

poorly aimed criticism aggravates employees who are always on time for work and who wonder why the warning about tardiness was not directed specifically to the problem employee.

A passive communication style quickly erodes the morale of even the best employees. It also results in a loss of trust and respect for the supervisor.

Not all supervisors who communicate passively are happy with the results of their communication efforts. In fact, when the desired behavior is not achieved, the passive communicator can begin to feel like a doormat who is disrespected and ignored. The pressure, frustration, and anger can build in the supervisor until at last their emotions explode over a seemingly trivial matter. The supervisor may recall a long list of disrespectful behaviors by employees in a rant. An employee witnessing the supervisor's meltdown is often left confused by the outburst, leading to a further loss of trust and respect.

Passive-Aggressive Communications. Supervisors who communicate in a passive-aggressive manner may avoid face-to-face conflict to give the illusion of a friendly, caring supervisor. But they differ from the passive communicator, who tries to avoid conflict altogether. The passive-aggressive supervisor's apparent passiveness, or even the occasional overly friendly image, serves as a cover for their "get even later" mentality.

A passive-aggressive supervisor could observe a behavior in a subordinate that he or she finds objectionable, yet the supervisor might remain silent about the behavior and might even engage the employee in friendly conversation. The employee would be left believing that nothing was wrong. The passive-aggressive supervisor might then report the observation of the objectionable behavior to his or her supervisor, hoping action would be taken against the employee. Passive-aggressive supervisors have even been known to pass problems to their supervisors anonymously in the form of unsigned written messages and photographs. Passive-aggressive supervisors have also passed the problem to their supervisor and then request that their supervisor not mention them when the issue is addressed with the subordinate.

If passive-aggressive supervisors can be described in one word, that word would be *manipulative*. They try to manipulate employees to like them through their friendliness and conflict avoidance, while manipulating their superiors to take actions against subordinates. Such supervisors are often experts at impression management. They have fooled many people over the years into believing that they are a decent person and one who is friendly and likable. Occasionally, passive-aggressive supervisors develop another disturbing skill. They can become masterful liars. They can lie and deny with a smile on their face, and some are so skilled at impression management that they fly under the radar of their own supervisors for years.

It is important to realize that it is not always supervisors who are passive-aggressive. Sometimes, subordinates have fine-tuned their passive-aggressive skills over several years. If you have a subordinate who is an expert at impression management (which is probably how he or she got the job in the first place) and is also a masterful liar, you have your hands full. You have a subordinate who has the skills to go over your head to your boss and convince your boss that you are wrong; they are right, and—you are picking on them.

There is no miracle cure for these subordinates. However, there are measures you can take to protect yourself. The best protection is documentation. Use supervisor's notes to document observed behaviors and the corrective measures taken by you to resolve any problems. It is much easier to defend yourself against accusations of *picking on* an employee if you have documentation showing your continuous efforts to help that employee. This is especially true for passive-aggressive individuals.

A final word of advice for those few supervisors who recognize that they might be passive-aggressive—make a change—today. Once the facade is gone and they see you for who you are, you will lose the trust of every employee.

Aggressive Communications. Supervisors who communicate aggressively do not care about the rights or feelings of others. Their communications may come across as being angry, loud, boisterous, and demeaning. Whether their mindset is well-meaning, but driven, to finish a task regardless of the costs to other's feelings, or whether they are motivated by some evil desire to rule over others as a bully or tyrant, the end results are the same. Their subordinates feel that such supervisors do not care about their needs, rights, or feelings.

Subordinates quickly realize that the easiest way to deal with an aggressive communicator is to avoid that supervisor. They seldom go to such supervisors with questions, concerns, or new ideas. An employee screamed at, yelled at, or embarrassed in public just once by a supervisor knows it is in their best interest to avoid that supervisor. Employees also learn quickly that if they are unfortunate enough to be forced to endure a long and demeaning lecture by an aggressive communicator, that they can easily tune out such supervisors. It is easy for employees to nod their head in compliant agreement without ever understanding the message the aggressive communicator is trying to relay.

Like the passive communicator, and the passive-aggressive communicator, the supervisor who uses an aggressive communication style is destined to lose the trust and respect of his or her subordinates. It is not an effective form of communication.

Assertive Communications. Supervisors who are assertive communicators say what they mean and mean what they say. And they find a way of communicating what they want without being mean. It is a relatively neutral tone, volume, and use of body language used for giving direction, or instruction, or clarifying a point, or asking or requiring an employee to meet a clearly stated expectation. Most assertive communication never needs to reach the point of being called an order, but it could include an order if necessary.

Assertive communicators can use common pleasantries such as, "Can you can take care of that for me?" If you fail to get the response you want from your initial assertive efforts, you can ramp up your assertiveness so that your request sounds more like a directive than a question. Assertiveness allows for some flexibility with the parameters being that there must be no mistake or misunderstanding the message you are trying to relay, and the way you deliver that message should not demean or embarrass the subordinate. It is as if you are standing up for your rights (those things you, as a supervisor, are entitled to ask for) without violating the rights of your subordinate.

Assertive communication is the communication style supervisors should strive to use as much as possible. It is effective at work and even at home. It removes, or strives to remove, all misunderstanding that is occasionally created through passive subtleties, or toxic aggressiveness. It allows for some flexibility depending on the situation to be slightly less or more assertive.

Assertive communicators have learned to be more direct in getting to their point and cutting out fluff that weakens the message or creates misunderstanding. Ideally, they learn how to be more direct without being uncomfortably blunt. They understand that yelling can feel demeaning to subordinates, but they also understand the appropriateness of raising and lowering vocal tone and volume to get their message across. They can incorporate humor, politeness, professionalism, respect for others, and the common human decency employees expect from those giving them direction or asking them to meet expectations.

Supervisors who are assertive communicators understand that their communication style is not about showing anyone that they are the boss. Your subordinates already know that you are their boss. Skilled supervisors use assertive communication to provide accurate and clear information, direction, and requests, and to minimize misunderstandings that are so common in supervisor-subordinate interactions.

R - Relationships

Work relationships are built one individual at a time. Like earning trust, building strong workplace relationships requires supervisors get to know the individuals they supervise. It is important for supervisors to learn what motivates individual employees. What are their career goals? What excites them both on and off the job? What are their interests, what is important to them, and what is their preferred communication style? Provide the same level of feedback to all employees and you are likely to get one that thinks you provide so little feedback that you do not care, and another who thinks you provide so much that you are a micromanager. Talk about career goals and one employee sees you as a mentor while another thinks you do not care about family because all you ever talk about is work.

Employees are individuals. Employees have different likes and dislikes, wants, and needs from the job. They even have different expectations from their supervisors. Relationship-building one individual at a time does not mean completing your efforts with one employee before moving on to the next. One individual at a time simply means getting to know your employees and then using the trust-earning and relationship-building skills that work best for you with that individual employee.

Learn what is important to your employees. Relationship building at work requires that you learn what is important to your employees and then have discussions about those subjects. Ask questions and then ask follow-up questions.

Rest assured; families are important to your employees. A supervisor who shows an interest in and concern for the well-being of an employee's family is well on his or her way to successful relationship building. It is also a safe bet that there are other things important to individual employees. Some are more interested in career advancement or professional development than others. Some employees love discussing their favorite hobby. One may enjoy discussing a new musical instrument they are learning to play. Another employee is proud of his new truck and would enjoy a conversation about that purchase.

Supervisors must attempt to discover what is important to their employees and then have occasional conversations about that subject. It does not matter if the subject interests the supervisor. Relationship building is not about the supervisor. What matters is that the supervisor shows an interest in subjects of interest to the employee.

Do not skip anyone. A police chief once told me he used all the strategies I discuss in this book, but said he found it was a lot easier if he skipped the people he did not like. He was right. It would be easier to skip certain people, but it would also be a mistake. Do not leave people out of your relationship-building efforts.

Building and maintaining solid relationships at work is easier with people you see as similar to yourself, and whom you like and like you in return. You like those who are respectful to you, and who do their jobs while making your job easier. You like having conversations

> *When it comes to your words and actions, make the same continuous relationship building efforts with all employees—even the ones you dislike. It is called work for a reason.*

with such employees. You engage with them regularly. You may even buy them a cup of coffee and never feel like you are doing it because it is your job. It just feels natural.

There are other employees who repeatedly undermine your leadership efforts, who talk about you behind your back, or whose personalities you find annoying. Continue trying to build a work relationship, even with those employees. The only difference between employees you like and dislike is that building trust with those you dislike feels like work. When it comes to your words and actions, make the same continuous relationship-building efforts with all employees—even the ones you dislike. It is called work for a reason.

How could you possibly try to build a strong working relationship with an employee you dislike? Let me first state for the record that it is not required that you like every employee. What is required is that you treat them fairly, professionally, and respectfully. And if you want even a chance at improving their performance (and making your life a little easier in the process) you need to try to build and maintain a strong work relationship. There are employees who like nothing better than to find some way of getting under your skin. But there is a phrase from an old television commercial about a deodorant that I would like you to consider. ***Never let them see you sweat.*** Do not give them the satisfaction by showing them they are getting to you. Work to build a solid workplace relationship.

There is another type of employee that supervisors tend to skip, and it has nothing to do with the fact that they like or dislike the employee. I am referring to the employee who is not a so-called direct report subordinate. You may encounter the subordinate on a different shift or in a different division and have no supervisory responsibilities over that employee. Nevertheless, these employees (and you) can benefit from a positive working relationship. Take the time to have conversations, to show you care about their work, and to show that you care about their well-being. They may not work directly for you today, but they may in the future, and they have long memories. Work to improve the work environment for everyone.

Workplace Gold

CHAPTER 19

Give Recognition

Trust is essential to building employee commitment. Giving recognition helps build trust. In fact, **recognition is the #1 performance accelerator**. Of all the leadership strategies discussed in this book, recognition is likely to result in the most performance improvement for the least amount of effort. Supervisors would be more likely to use recognition and see positive results from their efforts if they could remember this one simple rule:

> ### *What gets __recognized__ gets __repeated!__*

Giving recognition is an essential form of trust-building and employee engagement, and it should be part of every supervisor's continuous feedback efforts. Giving recognition shows your employees that their hard work matters, and that there is a difference between excellent and mediocre performance. Giving recognition also shows you care about employees as individuals.

What to Recognize

For far too long, supervisors have thought of recognition only in the context of awards and commendations. While commendations have a purpose, their use is limited to award-worthy circumstances. Some commendations come from acts of valor or meritorious actions. Some of those situations are a once-in-a-career event. Any leader would be happy (and lucky) to be able to give out such awards. Unfortunately, employees could go their entire career without circumstances occurring where they might merit such commendations.

The concept of *what gets recognized, gets repeated,* does not always work in award-worthy situations, because those occurrences are infrequent, if not rare. So, supervisors who want to build trust need to find ways to give recognition for circumstances that, while not necessarily award-worthy, are deserving of recognition. You can start your search for recognition-worthy occurrences by looking at both what your employees do and who they are as individuals.

Give recognition anytime an employee's results exceed your expectations. Give recognition when an employee simply meets your expectations but does so consistently, demonstrating their dependability. Give recognition anytime an employee shows improvement in any aspect of the job.

If you have an employee who is a poor report writer, and one day you get a report that shows improvement, give recognition for that improvement. It does not matter if the report is not perfect. It does not matter if the report is not as well-written as three other employees working the same shift. It only matters that there is improvement, that you are happy with the improvement, and that you would like to see the improvement repeated.

Give recognition anytime you see any behavior that you want repeated. It does not matter what the behavior is or even if your organization does not require the behavior. If the behavior is something you want more of, give recognition.

Give recognition to employees for their individual traits or characteristics that help make them a reliable employee and make your job as a supervisor just a little easier. Recognize employees that show leadership potential, that have integrity, a strong work ethic, a decent sense of humor, or who just make the job more enjoyable. *What gets recognized, gets repeated.*

Two ways to give recognition

1.   Your Words

Verbal Informal. The most effective (and easiest) form of recognition is verbal, in person, one-on-one between the supervisor and employee. It can be given anywhere and at any time either privately or in front of the employee's coworkers, whichever seems more appropriate for the circumstances.

Verbal Formal. Another form of verbal recognition is the formal public announcement. Some employees relish such public praise. Then again, not every circumstance warrants a formal announcement in front of the employee's coworkers. In addition, such public praise might even embarrass some employees. There is a time and place for formal public announcements. Make sure you know your employee well enough to know if this form of recognition is right for the employee and the situation.

Written Informal. A handwritten letter or note is an effective form of recognition. Today, emails and more formal letters written on a computer are so common that a handwritten note can feel more personal and often more meaningful. Copies of handwritten notes of recognition can be placed in personnel files—if the employee so desires. Often such notes are written just as a quick and personal way of saying thanks. Most employees realize such notes took a little more effort than a verbal "thank you" and appreciate the supervisor's effort.

Written Formal. It would be hard to deny that employees appreciate formal written letters or commendations that become a permanent part of their personnel file. If an incident is award-worthy or commendation-worthy, write that formal letter or commendation. For most employees (and their supervisors) those formal commendation moments occur too seldom to help the supervisor earn the employee's trust on a regular basis. But if the right circumstance occurs, give formal commendations whenever you have the opportunity.

Electronic. Electronic forms of recognition include telephone calls, text messages, and emails. Emails are especially useful but are frequently used too often when alternative forms of recognition would have been more appropriate. Email serves as a valid initial form of recognition, especially if you will not see your employee for the next couple days. Email also serves as a supplemental form of recognition after you have already given verbal recognition. Email even serves as a method to pass along your recognition to your supervisor (while copying the email to your employee).

Text messages can be a useful option. Text messaging can be used to show recognition or to say thanks for minor occurrences that once would have been ignored. So, while text messaging should not be used as a primary method of giving recognition, it is a valid supplemental option.

Finally, telephone calls are a valid option for delivering recognition. Although, it is important to know that telephone calls will never be as powerful or as meaningful as the supervisor delivering his or her recognition in person to the employee.

2. Your Actions

For many employees, actions speak louder than words. Assisting an employee can serve as a form of recognition. It could mean something as simple as asking an employee, "What could I do to make your job easier?" Maybe what your employee needs most is not your physical labor, but your ability to provide more resources (time, manpower, or equipment). Providing help could also mean helping the employee find a better, easier, or more efficient way to complete a task.

While providing help does not always mean pitching in to physically assist, occasionally that is exactly what is needed. I have heard from countless seminar attendees about excellent role models who were *not afraid to get their hands dirty.* But there is a big difference between helping and taking over. Taking over is likely to be viewed as micromanagement or perceived as you not trusting the employee. Try to find a balance between helping and taking over the task.

You can recognize an employee's leadership potential by granting them more responsibility. Typically, the more trust a supervisor shows an employee (and that includes granting them increased responsibility), the more trust and respect the supervisor gets in return. While assigning more responsibility may not be the right approach for every employee, it will work for many.

Providing career guidance to employees is a form of recognition for their past work efforts. Coaching and on-the-job skill development, especially at the immediate supervisor level, shows the employee that the supervisor cares about them and their career. Career mentoring, helping an employee identify his or her career interests—and suggesting a path to follow to make that interest a reality—is a powerful motivator, trust builder, and demonstration of recognition. Employees remember and stay loyal to their career mentors throughout their entire career.

Want to significantly multiply the effects of your recognition efforts?

Brag about the employee to others!

Pass the recognition along (in any format) to the employee's supervisor or to your boss!

Praise the employee in the media when appropriate and possible.

Finally, providing, recommending, or suggesting formal professional development opportunities is seen by many employees as recognition by their supervisor for having done a good job. Not every employee seeks professional development, but for some, professional development is very important. A supervisor who can recommend, or provide, the training opportunity is in a position to provide a meaningful form of recognition to the employee. Like career mentoring, professional development can result in career-long commitment to an individual supervisor.

The Five Bs of Recognition
Once you decide to give an employee recognition for what they do or who they are, make that effort count. Recognition opportunities do not come along every day. Too often, those opportunities are missed, and even when they occur, delivery of the recognition is often mismanaged. When delivering employee recognition, consider *The Five Bs of Recognition*.

1. Be Specific
To be effective, recognition must be specific. Tell employees specifically what they did that was any different from all the other days they showed up for work when no one offered a comment. Telling someone they did a *good job* is better than no recognition at all, but not by much. Tell them specifically what they did right so that the behavior gets repeated.

2. Be Sincere
Recognition will feel insincere if it is given for no valid reason, or is exaggerated, or is given to employees who did not earn it—just to make a self-serving supervisor look good. Approach your employees individually and tell them specifically what they did that you appreciate (and would like to see repeated).

Timing matters. Leaving the room then returning to give recognition as an afterthought gives the impression that it was not that important. Give recognition when you have time to state what and why you are giving the recognition and do it at a place and at a time where it will be best received by the employee.

The words you choose matter, and how you say them matters. Humor is occasionally acceptable, but do not dilute the importance of the recognition with jokes or sarcasm. Supervisors should also be cautious in their use of vocal tone and body language. When, where, and how you deliver your words of recognition are every bit as important as the words themselves—and maybe more so in some cases.

3. Be Timely
Ideally, recognition should be given immediately after the circumstances that merit the recognition (or as soon as possible) if it is to have any value. The closer to the event that you can give recognition, the more power your words will have in building trust. If you cannot provide in-person recognition for a few hours or days, use electronic forms of communication such as telephone calls, text messages, or emails to contact the employee. Whenever you use electronic communication to deliver recognition, follow it up in person as soon as possible.

4. Be Personal
Make your recognition efforts as personal as possible. That means make it about the deserving employee. Do not include those not even marginally involved in the recognition-worthy situation. At times, supervisors are so afraid of leaving someone out that they include everyone

and end up alienating the person who is most deserving of the recognition.

In addition, employees may like to receive recognition in different forms. Some may like their recognition-worthy deed announced to the entire agency at the next roll call. Others would be embarrassed to tears if that occurred. Some employees would love to see their name in the local paper for a recognition-worthy incident. Some would be happy for just a few kind words from a supervisor they trust and respect. The supervisor who learns to give recognition in a manner best suited for an individual employee will receive the most trust and commitment in return.

Use multiple forms of recognition. Giving verbal recognition in person does not mean you are prevented from following up with some form of written or electronic recognition. And if you give written or electronic recognition first, follow it up with in-person verbal recognition. While giving multiple forms of recognition, do not forget to pass along the recognition to your supervisor. While it is terrific that you know your employee is doing an excellent job, it may be even more beneficial for the employee (and you) if your supervisor knows your employee is doing an excellent job.

Finally, you may occasionally find yourself so busy with emergencies and day-to-day activities that you forget to give recognition when you had the best intention of delivering it either in person or as a formal commendation. If you forget, apologize for forgetting (especially if you told the employee you would write a commendation) and then correct the situation. It is never too late to give recognition.

5. Be Frequent

Whatever form of recognition you chose to deliver, find opportunities to give it often. Do not wait for the big lifesaving media event. You could be waiting a long time. Most departments have policies and procedures regarding a formal awards program. Such programs serve a purpose, but they do not prevent supervisors from giving recognition in circumstances that may not rise to the level of an award-worthy event as defined by department policy.

A noticeable improvement in the writing ability shown in an officer's report, the recovery of contraband on a traffic stop because of excellent observational skills, or the way an officer professionally calms down an irate member of the public are all minor incidents that may not be award-worthy. However, they are all circumstances or behaviors that any supervisor would be happy to see repeated in an employee. Too often, supervisors miss recognition-worthy moments waiting for the big event that never occurs. Do not miss those trust building opportunities.

CHAPTER 20

There Will Be Days

Real-world law enforcement means real-world problems. Making tough leadership decisions is not about democracy, and such decisions are not about popularity. From time to time leadership strategies that looked great in a book or sounded great in a classroom get stalled by circumstances when supervisors attempt to apply them in real life. Do not become frustrated in your efforts to build trust and earn employee commitment because a situation arises that seems to stall your well-intentioned efforts.

Even as you make gradual changes to improve the work environment by building trust, holding employees accountable, communicating more clearly, and giving recognition, there will be setbacks. There will be moments, maybe entire days, when you are so busy you miss opportunities to engage with employees. It is possible on those days that some employees might misread your focus on work as you being aloof or uncaring.

There will be days when emergency situations or critical incidents occur that require your full attention. It is possible on some of those days that your demeanor may come across to a few of your employees as that of command-and-control micromanager who cares only about the job, and not about employees.

There will be days when you are so busy that you view a problem brought to your attention as so minor as to not merit your time. Maybe you meant to address the problem later, but you were so busy you forgot. As a result, some employees might label you as a conflict-avoidance boss who is not up to the challenges of the job.

There will be days when you are dealing with a problem employee and everyone seems to have an opinion on how you should handle the situation. Some employees insist that you should hand out the harshest discipline possible. Other employees come to the problem employee's defense and believe you are overreacting to the situation.

There will be days when you hope an exemplary employee you are mentoring gets promoted, but you learn that your boss promoted another candidate. It is hard watching someone you are trying to help lose out, become disappointed and angry, and watch their attitude take at least a temporary dive. They might even lose a little faith in your ability to help and mentor their career. At the same time, you try to help that employee, another perceives your efforts towards that employee as favoritism.

There will be days when an employee you like and have a high degree of trust with does something stupid. Believe it or not, on occasion, even good employees do stupid things. You may get pressure from subordinates and supervisors alike to impose stern consequences. Their pressure can even cause you to become angry at the employee, and in a moment of lost temper you might say hurtful words that are quickly relayed by coworkers back to the employee. Years of building trust can be lost in a matter of seconds.

There will be days when you think you are doing the right things, you are using the strategies in this book, plus those you have picked up over the years, but you feel you are getting nothing in return. You see no immediate improvement. You still hear from the chronic complainers and the morale killers, but you hear nothing from your outstanding employees. It can become very frustrating.

There will be days when you have repeatedly, but unsuccessfully tried to make a connection and build trust with one employee. You feel you have tried to meet the employee halfway and have gotten nothing in return. Understand that what you consider halfway and what the employee considers halfway may be vastly different. Plus, know that when it comes to leadership efforts, halfway is seldom enough.

Employees will not always vocalize (at least not to you) the degree of trust and respect they have for you today. They will be quick to let you know if they are unhappy, but satisfied employees may remain silent—at least until your retirement party. Know that if most of your employees are doing their job while treating each other with respect, plus they seem to enjoy coming to work most days—you are on the right track.

On those days when things do not seem to go right, as sometimes happens in law enforcement, view those frustrating days as temporary setbacks or speed bumps, not as roadblocks. Keep moving forward. No one ever said doing the right thing would be easy. The concepts in this book are simple, but simple is not always easy. Even the most basic leadership strategies require effort to apply. Make the effort. Make a difference in the lives of your employees. That is what authentic leaders do!

<u>About the Author</u>

Ron developed his passion for both training and leadership while assigned as an instructor at the Coast Guard Training Center on Governor's Island, NY.

Following his enlistment, he began his police career in Massachusetts as a patrol officer. Later as a patrol sergeant, he served as his department's training officer. Ron eventually accepted a position as police chief and served in that position for 17 years. During his tenure as chief, Ron completed his master's degree in criminal justice and worked as an adjunct instructor at a regional police academy teaching everything from legal issues to leadership. Later in his police career, Ron worked as an instructor and subsequently served as president of the Municipal Police Institute, where he developed and taught leadership courses.

After more than 26 years in law enforcement, Ron retired in 2011 and began traveling the country presenting his leadership strategies to law enforcement organizations. He is a frequent speaker at the International Association of Chiefs of Police conference and has presented at numerous other law enforcement training conferences. His practical solutions to common employee problems have established his reputation as an authority on employee accountability and performance. Ron and his wife reside on Cape Cod (Massachusetts).

Speaker Information and Book Orders

Ron is available for association conference presentations, and training at individual agencies throughout the country. If you would like additional information about scheduling Ron as a speaker, or if you would like to order additional copies of this book, please contact:

Ronald C. Glidden
Glidden Training & Consulting, LLC
P.O. Box 73
South Wellfleet, MA 02663

Email: chief@ronglidden.com
Website: www.ronglidden.com

Ron's Other Books

52 Bulletproof Leadership Tips, Volume 1
52 Bulletproof Leadership Tips, Volume 2
52 Bulletproof Leadership Tips, Volume 3
52 Bulletproof Leadership Tips, Volume 4
52 Bulletproof Leadership Tips, Volume 5
Stopping the School Shooter

Sign up to receive your FREE weekly *Bulletproof Leadership Tips*

If you are not already a subscriber, sign up today to receive your FREE weekly *Bulletproof Leadership Tips* by email. These tips are delivered to your email inbox every Wednesday morning.

To subscribe, just go to www.RonGlidden.com and click on the subscription button.